USELESS INFORMATION

Anthony Quinn 60¢

THE WORLD'S GREATEST BOOK OF
USELESS
INFORMATION

If You Thought You Knew All the Things You
Didn't Need to Know—Think Again

NOEL BOTHAM

AND THE USELESS INFORMATION SOCIETY

A PERIGEE BOOK

A PERIGEE BOOK
Published by the Penguin Group
Penguin Group (USA) Inc.
375 Hudson Street, New York, New York 10014, USA
Penguin Group (Canada), 90 Eglinton Avenue East, Suite 700, Toronto, Ontario M4P 2Y3, Canada
(a division of Pearson Penguin Canada Inc.)
Penguin Books Ltd., 80 Strand, London WC2R 0RL, England
Penguin Group Ireland, 25 St. Stephen's Green, Dublin 2, Ireland (a division of Penguin Books Ltd.)
Penguin Group (Australia), 250 Camberwell Road, Camberwell, Victoria 3124, Australia
(a division of Pearson Australia Group Pty. Ltd.)
Penguin Books India Pvt. Ltd., 11 Community Centre, Panchsheel Park, New Delhi—110 017, India
Penguin Group (NZ), 67 Apollo Drive, Rosedale, North Shore 0632, New Zealand
(a division of Pearson New Zealand Ltd.)
Penguin Books (South Africa) (Pty.) Ltd., 24 Sturdee Avenue, Rosebank, Johannesburg 2196,
South Africa

Penguin Books Ltd., Registered Offices: 80 Strand, London WC2R 0RL, England

While the author has made every effort to provide accurate telephone numbers and Internet addresses at
the time of publication, neither the publisher nor the author assumes any responsibility for errors, or for
changes that occur after publication. Further, the publisher does not have any control over and does not
assume any responsibility for author or third-party websites or their content.

First edition: July 2009

Library of Congress Cataloging-in-Publication Data

Botham, Noel, 1940–
  The world's greatest book of useless information : if you thought you knew all the things you didn't
need to know, think again / Noel Botham.—1st ed.
    p. cm.
  ISBN 978-0-399-53502-4
  1. Curiosities and wonders.   2. Handbooks, vade mecums, etc.   I. Useless Information Society.
II. Title.
  AG243.B665 2009
  031.02—dc22
                                                                    2009003589

PRINTED IN THE UNITED STATES OF AMERICA

10   9   8   7   6   5   4   3   2   1

Most Perigee books are available at special quantity discounts for bulk purchases for sales promotions,
premiums, fund-raising, or educational use. Special books, or book excerpts, can also be created to fit spe-
cific needs. For details, write: Special Markets, Penguin Group (USA) Inc., 375 Hudson Street, New York,
New York 10014.

Members of the Useless Information Society

Chairman
NOEL BOTHAM
General Secretary
KEITH WATERHOUSE
Beadle
KENNY CLAYTON
Chaplain
FATHER MICHAEL SEED
MICHAEL DILLON
BRIAN HITCHEN
ALASDAIR LONG
TIM WOODWARD
RICHARD LITTLEJOHN
STEVE WALSH
STRUAN RODGER
GAVIN HANS-HAMILTON
ASHLEY LUFF

SUGGS
MIKE MALLOY
MICHAEL BOOTH
JOHN PAYNE
BARRY PALIN
JOSEPH CONNOLLY
TONY COBB
JOHN MCENTEE
JOHN BLAKE
JOHN ROBERTS
BILL HAGGARTY
CHARLES LOWE
JOHN KING
KEN STOTT
RICHARD CORRIGAN
CONNER WALSH
JOHN TAYLOR

CONTENTS

THE CREATIVE CULTURE

WHAT'S IN A NAME?

Michael Keaton's real name is Michael Douglas.

Dirk Bogarde's real name is Derek Jules Gaspard Ulric Niven van den Bogarde.

Jane Seymour's real name is Joyce Penelope Wilhelmina Frankenberg.

Sting's real name is Gordon Matthew Thomas Sumner.

Mickey Rooney's real name is Joseph Yule Jr.

Wonder Woman's real name is Diana Prince.

The real name of Batman villain the Penguin is Oswald Cobblepot.

Billie Holiday was known as Lady Day.

In 1925, MGM ran a contest to find a new name for Lucille LeSueur. They settled on Joan Crawford.

The heavy metal band Black Sabbath got their name from a 1963 horror film of the same name, starring Boris Karloff.

The names of the six Gummi bears are Gruffi, Cubbi, Tummi, Zummi, Sunni, and Grammi.

Billy Batson must say the name of the ancient wizard Shazam to transform into Captain Marvel.

The Pac-Man video arcade game featured colored ghosts named Inky, Blinky, Pinky, and Clyde.

Some Like It Hot was originally called *Not Tonight, Josephine.*

The names of Popeye's four nephews are Pipeye, Peepeye, Pupeye, and Poopeye.

The Hitchcock film *North by Northwest* takes its name from a *Hamlet* quote: "I am but mad north-northwest."

The Muppet Miss Piggy was originally named Miss

Piggy Lee as homage to singer Peggy Lee. The name was eventually changed to Miss Piggy to avoid upsetting the singer.

THE RESERVATION IS UNDER . . .

Some memorable pseudonyms celebrities have used at hotels:

Elizabeth Hurley—Rebecca de Winter

Jon Bon Jovi—Stanley Kowalski

Marlon Brando—Lord Greystoke, aka Tarzan

Angelina Jolie—Miss Lollipop

Jennifer Aniston—Mrs. Smith

Val Kilmer—Thomas Paine

Paris Hilton—Tinkerbell

George Clooney—Arnold Schwarzenegger

Bono—J. C. Penney

Britney Spears—Bella

Kate Beckinsale—Sigourney Beaver (although her husband is not a fan of being called "Mr. Beaver")

O. J. Simpson—D. H. Lawrence

IN PRODUCTION

Paramount is the only major movie studio still based in Hollywood.

One of the actors in *Reservoir Dogs*, Eddie Bunker, was a real former criminal and was once on the FBI's Ten Most Wanted list.

The first film to show the sex act was *Extase* in 1932.

The longest interval between an original film and its sequel is forty-six years—between *The Wizard of Oz* and *Return to Oz*.

Judy Garland was sixteen years old when she appeared in *The Wizard of Oz*.

A record 8,552 animals were featured in *Around the World in Eighty Days*.

On the set of *The Usual Suspects*, Kevin Spacey glued his fingers together to keep his left hand consistently paralyzed.

Roger Moore and Daniel Craig are the only English actors to have played the role of James Bond. Sean Connery is Scottish, George Lazenby is Australian, Timothy Dalton is Welsh, and Pierce Brosnan is Irish.

Thora Birch was only seventeen during filming of *American Beauty*, so her nude scene had to be filmed in the presence of her parents and child labor representatives.

Humphrey Bogart ad-libbed *Casablanca*'s classic line "Here's looking at you, kid."

The companies responsible for the end of the world in the *Terminator* movies, Skynet and Cyberdyne Systems, actually exist.

The roar of the Tyrannosaurus rex in *Jurassic Park* is actually the sound of the aircraft simulator at NASA's Langley Research Center.

TECHNICAL DIFFICULTIES

The largest number of fatalities on a film set is forty, occurring during the making of *The Sword of Tipu Sultan*.

In *Gladiator*, during the initial Colosseum fight of Rome versus Carthage, one of the chariots crashes into a wall, revealing an air tank in the back.

In *Zulu*, some of the Zulu warriors are blatantly wearing the wristwatches they were paid with.

In *Superman*, when Superman discovers Lois Lane's body he lets out a scream, revealing his tooth fillings.

In *Star Wars*, when the stormtroopers break into the control room where R2-D2 and C-3PO are hiding, one of them hits his head on the doorway.

ERRORS IN JUDGMENT

MGM's Irving Thalberg rejected *Gone with the Wind*, saying, "No Civil War picture ever made a nickel!"

Henry Winkler, aka the Fonz in *Happy Days*, turned down the role of Danny Zuko in *Grease*.

Tom Selleck was originally cast as Indiana Jones but turned down the role to star in *Magnum, P.I.*

HOLLYWOOD HISTORY

The Hollywood sign originally read "Hollywoodland."

Norma Talmadge (accidentally) made the first footprints in the forecourt of Grauman's Chinese Theatre in May 1927.

As well as the handprints and footprints outside Grauman's Chinese Theatre, there are also casts of Groucho Marx's cigar, Betty Grable's legs, Jimmy Durante's nose, Harold Lloyd's glasses, and Whoopi Goldberg's braids.

Darth Vader has advertised Duracell batteries.

Disney Studios has the record for the biggest global box-office year of all time, grossing more than $3 billion in 2003.

August 29, 1997, is the date of Judgment Day in *Terminator 2*.

The *Braveheart* sword was auctioned in Hollywood in 2001 for $170,000.

The 1978 TV series *Battlestar Galactica* was the subject of lawsuits from 20th Century Fox, as the company alleged it was a "steal" from *Star Wars*.

The soap opera *The Bold and the Beautiful* had quite a predicament when it killed off heroine Caroline Forrester in 1990, considering that in Italy, the show was called *Caroline* and was the number one show of all time. Disaster was averted by renaming the show *Beautiful*.

AWARDS SEASON

Less than 250 people attended the first-ever Academy Awards ceremony, which lasted fifteen minutes, with tickets costing just five dollars.

Disney's *Beauty and the Beast* is the only animated film ever to be nominated for a Best Picture Oscar.

Since 1989, to avoid offending losers, Oscar presenters

say, "And the Oscar goes to . . ." instead of "And the winner is . . ."

An Oscar statuette weighs 8.5 pounds and stands at 13.5 inches tall.

Comedian, director, actor, and author Billy Crystal has won three Emmy awards for hosting the Academy Awards.

Bob Hope hosted the Academy Awards a record eighteen times.

The Academy Awards ceremony has never been canceled, only postponed.

Two actors have won Tony awards for playing the opposite sex in a role: Mary Martin in 1955 for *Peter Pan* and Harvey Fierstein in 2003 for *Hairspray*.

STARS—THEY'RE JUST LIKE US . . .

Brad Pitt once worked as a chicken for the El Pollo Loco restaurant chain.

Meryl Streep, Dustin Hoffman, Gene Hackman, and Burt Lancaster all started out as waitstaff.

Oliver Reed was once a bouncer for a strip club.

While attending Juilliard with Val Kilmer, Kevin Spacey borrowed money from Kilmer's parents and never paid it back.

SOMETIMES . . .

Elizabeth Taylor and Richard Burton first married in Canada in 1964, and then again in Botswana in 1975.

The shortest ever Hollywood marriage is the six-hour union of Rudolph Valentino and Jean Acker.

Goldie Hawn and Kurt Russell had a car stolen from their driveway and didn't notice for three days.

After breaking up with his fiancée Winona Ryder, Johnny Depp had his tattoo "Winona Forever" changed to "Wino Forever."

Meryl Streep has stated that when she auditioned for Jessica Lange's part in the 1976 remake of *King Kong*, the producer asked, in Italian, "Why did you send me this pig? This woman is so ugly!" Streep, fluent in the language, supposedly answered back, "I'm very sorry to disappoint you."

THE ARTISTS' WAY

War photographer Robert Capa's famous photos of D-Day were selected from only eleven exposures that survived the developing process. Although he had shot four rolls of film, most of the photos were ruined by heat.

Michelangelo was harshly criticized by a Vatican official for the nudity in his fresco *The Last Judgement*, which hangs on the walls of the Sistine Chapel in Rome. In retaliation the artist made some changes to his work: he painted in the face of the complaining clergyman as the judge of the underworld.

When he was young Leonardo da Vinci supposedly drew a picture of a horrible monster and placed it near a window in order to surprise his father. The drawing was so convincing that, upon seeing it, his father believed it to be real and set out to protect his family until the boy showed him it was just a picture. Da Vinci's father then enrolled his son in an art class.

In Leonardo da Vinci's famous painting *The Last Supper*, a salt cellar near Judas Iscariot is knocked over. This is said to have started the superstition that spilled salt is unlucky.

X-rays of Leonardo da Vinci's *Mona Lisa* revealed there to be three completely different versions of the same subject, all painted by da Vinci, under the final portrait.

Paul Cézanne was fifty-six years old when he had his first one-man exhibition.

The Thinker, a sculpture by Auguste Rodin, was originally named *The Poet* as it was meant to depict the poet Dante.

Whistler's best-known painting, often called *Whistler's Mother*, is actually titled *Arrangement in Grey and Black: The Artist's Mother*.

Ancient Chinese artists freely painted scenes of nakedness but wouldn't depict a bare female foot.

In 2008, an Austrian art group erected a two-hundred-foot-long pink bunny on a mountainside in Italy. The bunny, which was knit out of pink wool, can be seen from space and will remain on the mountain until 2025. The group expects hikers to climb up twenty feet to its soft belly to relax.

MUSICAL NOTES

It's been estimated that an opera singer burns an average of more than two calories per minute during a performance.

The harp's ancestor is a hunting bow.

Violins weigh less than sixteen ounces yet resist string tension of more than sixty-five pounds.

The oldest piano still in existence was built in 1720 by the Italian instrument maker Bartolomeo Cristofori.

A total of 364 gifts are given by the lover in the song "The Twelve Days of Christmas."

Seventy-five percent of people who play the car radio while driving also sing along with it.

Contralto is the deepest female singing voice.

James Dean recorded an album called *Jungle Rhythm*.

Chopin made his debut as a pianist at the age of eight.

Tchaikovsky was financed by a wealthy widow for thirteen years. At her request, they never met.

Mozart once composed a piano piece that required a player to use two hands and a nose in order to hit all the correct notes.

Only one person walked with Mozart's coffin from the church to the cemetery for its burial.

In 1600, the loudest sound that could be made was that of a pipe organ.

Italian composer Gioacchino Antonio Rossini covered himself with blankets when he composed, and could only find inspiration by getting profoundly drunk.

Johann Sebastian Bach once walked 230 miles to hear the organist at Lubeck in Germany.

Handel wrote the score of his *Messiah* in just over three weeks.

The composer Richard Wagner, a vegetarian, once published a diatribe against "the abominable practice of flesh eating."

Ludwig van Beethoven was once arrested for vagrancy.

Irving Berlin composed three thousand songs in his lifetime but couldn't read music.

Dolly Parton owns a theme park called Dollywood in the Great Smoky Mountains of Tennessee.

Bruce Willis once played with his band at the opening of a branch of Krispy Kreme Doughnuts.

The Fine Young Cannibals won Best British Group at the 1990 Brit Awards. But the band members returned their trophies, saying that the awards show was being used to promote Margaret Thatcher.

Johnny Cash recorded an album live in Folsom State Prison, in California.

The 27 Club is a pop culture name for a group of influential musicians who all died at the age of twenty-seven, including Kurt Cobain, Janis Joplin, Jimi Hendrix, and Jim Morrison. Actor River Phoenix could also be included in this group since he was also a musician.

LONG LIVE THE KING

In October 1945, at age ten, Elvis Presley won second prize in a talent contest by singing the tearjerker "Old Shep" at the Mississippi-Alabama Fair and Dairy Show in Tupelo.

Elvis's mother bought him his first guitar at a Tupelo hardware store as a present for his eleventh birthday. Elvis wanted a bicycle.

Elvis's first girlfriend was sixteen-year-old Dixie Locke, a high school senior who was his first prom date.

In 1957, at age twenty-two, Elvis bought Graceland. He paid $100,000 for the property.

Elvis recorded more than 650 songs—eighteen of his singles reaching number one in the charts. With a three-octave voice, his number-one hits covered a range of styles, including country, gospel, rock 'n' roll, rhythm and blues, and pop.

"Heartbreak Hotel" was originally penned by steel guitarist Tommy Durden and high school teacher Mae Boren Axton.

Actress Jana Lund was the first woman to kiss Elvis

on film, in his second movie, *Loving You*. It was also his first color movie. The movie was a family affair; both his mother and father appeared in the production as audience members.

Elvis's favorite costar was supposedly Shelley Fabares, who appeared in three of his films.

If he wanted to book seats or travel incognito, Elvis frequently used the names Dr. John Carpenter or John Burrows Jr.

Elvis was a big animal lover and his many pets at Graceland included cats, dogs, ducks, fish, ponies, peacocks, a parrot, and a chimpanzee.

Major Bill Smith, a record producer who met Elvis in 1956, says he talked to Elvis after his supposed death and received two remarkable cassettes in the mail, allegedly sent by the King. A police voice identification expert from Houston compared one of the tapes with an Elvis interview from 1962 and found a staggering thirty-five instances where the voice patterns matched.

SO YOU THINK YOU CAN DANCE

The name of the waltz comes from the German word *waltzen*, meaning "to revolve."

Kazatsky is a Russian folk dance characterized by a step in which a squatting dancer kicks out each leg alternately to the front.

The fox-trot was named for music writer Harry Fox.

There are five basic foot positions in ballet.

Merrill Ashley holds the record for the longest performance career with the New York City Ballet, at thirty years.

George Balanchine and Mikhail Baryshnikov were both born in January.

Traditional Highland dances were meant to be danced only by men. The Highland fling, the oldest, was a fertility dance based on the rutting movements of the stag.

The earliest dance marathon was held in England in 1364. The longest recorded marathon lasted twenty-two weeks, three days.

TOON TALES

The cartoon strip "Peanuts" has appeared in some 2,600 newspapers in seventy-five countries, and has been translated into twenty-one languages. It is known as "Radishes" in Denmark.

Dennis the Menace lives in Wichita, Kansas.

Minnie Mouse rejected Mickey Mouse's advances in

their first film together by parachuting out of an airplane when he tried to kiss her.

The Japanese cartoon *Sazae-san* has aired every Sunday since 1969.

One difference between animated chipmunks Chip 'n' Dale is that Chip has one tooth and Dale has two.

CURTAIN CALL

The taboo against whistling backstage at a theater comes from the pre-electricity era, when a whistle was the signal for the curtains and the scenery to drop. An unexpected whistle could have caused an unexpected scene change.

If an actor refers to *Macbeth* by name while in the theater, he must spin around in a circle three times, while saying a line from the show, and spit.

Any unexplainable mischief that befalls a production is likely to be blamed on Thespis, especially if it happens on November 23. On what has been estimated to be November 23, 534 BCE, Thespis of ancient Athens was the first person to speak lines as an individual actor on stage.

The musical *The Phantom of the Opera* has grossed more than $3 billion since 1986 and is the longest-running musical on Broadway.

Plans for a sequel to *The Phantom of the Opera* were delayed when composer Andrew Lloyd Webber's cat climbed onto his digital piano and managed to delete the entire score.

AD SPACE

There are twenty thousand television commercials made each year that are aimed exclusively at children, seven thousand of them for sugared breakfast cereals.

The average American is exposed to approximately three thousand advertisements a day.

The drug company Bayer was once plagued by a hoaxer who created a fake ad in Egypt showing a mother roasting a baby over a fire, with a tagline reading, "Heals their burn and your guilt, fast."

In the mornings in Japan, free tissues are handed to bus and rail commuters by workers of the companies who print messages and advertisements on them. Most public bathrooms do not have paper towels or toilet paper.

BOOK FAIR

FIRST DRAFTS

Scarlett O'Hara, Margaret Mitchell's *Gone with the Wind* heroine, was originally given the name Pansy.

The original title of Jane Austen's novel *Pride and Prejudice* was *First Impressions*. Her book *Northanger Abbey* was originally called *Susan*.

Jacqueline Susann's bestselling novel *Valley of the Dolls* was originally titled *They Don't Build Statues to Businessmen*.

Catch-22, by Joseph Heller, was originally titled *Catch-18* in a magazine excerpt.

F. Scott Fitzgerald's *Great Gatsby* was originally titled *Incident at West Egg*.

Leo Tolstoy's wife had to copy manuscripts of both *War and Peace* and *Anna Karenina* by hand. Tolstoy considered *Anna Karenina*, not *War and Peace*, to be his first attempt at a novel.

Victor Hugo wrote *The Hunchback of Notre Dame* in just six months and, it is said, with a single bottle of ink.

Dr. Samuel Johnson wrote the story "Rasselas" in one week so he could earn the money to pay for his mother's funeral.

NOMS DE PLUME

George Eliot's real name was Mary Ann Evans.

Winnie, from A. A. Milne's *Winnie the Pooh*, was named after his son's teddy bear. The child named his toy after "Winnipeg," a bear he often saw at the London Zoo.

Created by author Astrid Lindgren, the children's book character Pippi Longstocking's full name is Pippilotta Delicatessa Windowshade Mackrelmint Ephraimsdaughter Longstocking.

Before he settled on the name Mark Twain, writer Samuel Clemens published work under the names Thomas Jefferson Snodgrass, Sergeant Fathom, and W. Apaminondas Adrastus Blab.

Fagin, the celebrated villain in Charles Dickens's *Oliver*

Twist, was also the name of Dickens's best friend, Bob Fagin.

- Russian writer Konstantin Mikhailov had 325 pseudonyms.

LITERARY SCANDAL

Agatha Christie created a mystery herself by disappearing for eleven days in 1926, only to be discovered at a Harrogate Hydro hotel.

D. H. Lawrence's novel *Lady Chatterley's Lover* was the subject of an obscenity trial in Britain in 1959.

The Soviet Union banned Sir Arthur Conan Doyle's *Adventures of Sherlock Holmes* because of the book's references to occultism and spiritualism.

Emile Zola had two families, with his wife and his mistress, and they all lived in the same house together.

In the seventeenth century there once lived a real-life Doctor Frankenstein. Physician Konrad Johann Dippel set up a laboratory at Frankenstein Castle, near Darmstat, Germany, where he could pursue his hobby of alchemy. Like Frankenstein, Dippel was also interested in the possibility of immortality through scientific means, and exhumed corpses from Frankenstein's cemetery to experiment on. When the townspeople started to suspect him of stealing corpses, he turned to trying the experiments on himself, and died drinking one of his formulas.

William Ireland once forged a new version of *King Lear* and various other documents supposedly written by Shakespeare. He then wrote a story called "Voltigern," which he claimed was a lost Shakespearean play. Many scholars examined the documents and declared them to be authentic, but when the play was performed on stage it was so terrible that it was booed off.

Lord Byron was rumored to have impregnated his half sister.

Playwright Richard Brinsley Sheridan was such a compulsive drinker that he would drink eau de cologne.

When the British painter and poet Rossetti's wife died, he decided to bury his book, *Poems by D. Rossetti*, with her. Years later, he exhumed his poems from his wife's grave.

During the Chinese Cultural Revolution, all literary works by Charles Dickens and William Shakespeare were banned.

William Prynne, the British pamphleteer, had his ears cut off because of his inflammatory publications.

🌰 RATED PG

Hans Christian Andersen's *Wonder Stories* was banned from children's reading lists in Illinois due to a suggestive illustration that might encourage children to break dishes so they didn't have to dry them.

On a related note, Shel Silverstein's children's book *A Light in the Attic* has been banned in many schools and libraries for inappropriate content, one particular complaint being that the poem "How Not to Have to Dry the Dishes" encourages messiness and disobedience in children.

Harriet the Spy, by Louise Fitzhugh, has been banned in parts of the United States for teaching children to lie, spy, talk back, and curse.

WHAT'S A SYNONYM FOR "ECCENTRIC"?

D. H. Lawrence enjoyed taking off his clothes and climbing mulberry trees.

Emily Dickinson was a recluse by the age of thirty, dressing only in white and carrying on friendships through correspondence.

James Joyce suffered from stomach ulcers most of his life and believed that the key to good health was defecation, and if he didn't get to perform the act at least three times a day he would fret. He was so fascinated by stools that he once asked his wife, Nora, to defecate on a piece of paper while he lay down underneath her and observed.

Edgar Rice Burroughs wrote twenty-six *Tarzan* books without ever visiting Africa.

Beatrix Potter, famous for writing and illustrating the Peter Rabbit children's books, actually had a rabbit killed with chloroform to provide the model for Peter Rabbit.

Lord Byron had four pet geese that he took everywhere with him, even to social gatherings.

After the death of her husband, poet Percy Shelley, Mary Shelley kept his heart in her desk.

Henrik Ibsen kept a picture of his archrival August Strindberg hanging over his desk to inspire him to work harder.

In Denmark, an author who wrote a book criticizing the Swedes, who were at that time occupying his country, was arrested and then given the choice of either being beheaded or eating his own words. He opted to eat his own words by boiling his book in broth and making a soup out of it.

Robert Browning used Chianti to wean and cure his wife, Elizabeth Barrett Browning, from her addiction to laudanum.

Dr. Seuss wrote *Green Eggs and Ham* after his editor dared him to write a book using fewer than fifty different words.

Robert Louis Stevenson said he had envisioned the story *The Strange Case of Dr. Jekyll and Mr. Hyde* in a dream and simply recorded it the way he saw it. Stevenson claimed to be able to dream plots for his stories at will.

Rudyard Kipling would only write when he had black ink in his pen.

Between 1986 and 1996, Brazilian author Jose Carlos Ryoki de Alpoim Inoue had 1,058 novels published.

Norwegian playwright Henrik Ibsen had a pet scorpion that he kept on his desk for inspiration.

Charles Dickens always touched things three times for luck.

Charles Dickens would work himself up so much when he performed his own works on stage that he sometimes fainted.

Marcel Proust had a pet swordfish.

D. H. Lawrence would only make love in the dark.

Dostoyevsky and F. Scott Fitzgerald both had foot fetishes.

MOONLIGHTING

James Bond author Ian Fleming also wrote the children's novel *Chitty Chitty Bang Bang*.

Margaret Mitchell wrote the novel *Gone with the Wind* as she was bored while recuperating from a sprained ankle.

Danielle Steel is a descendant of the Löwenbrau brewery family and worked for a PR firm before becoming a novelist.

Lewis Carroll was a mathematics professor at Oxford University. After reading *Alice in Wonderland*, Queen Victoria sent a letter to him asking for another of his books to read. Carroll sent her a book on algebra.

Ernest Hemingway drove an ambulance during World War I.

The young Charles Dickens wanted to be an actor.

George Orwell worked as a policeman before turning to a writing career.

Anthony Trollope invented the pillar-box (a pillar-shaped mailbox in the United Kingdom).

The great lover and adventurer Casanova was earning his living as a librarian for a count in Bohemia when he wrote his memoirs.

Winston Churchill's *History of the English-Speaking Peoples* was published when he was eighty-two years old.

Rudyard Kipling was fired as a reporter for the *San Francisco Examiner*. His dismissal letter said, "I'm sorry, Mr. Kipling, but you just don't know how to use the English language. This isn't a kindergarten for amateur writers."

BOOK WORMS

The Indian epic poem the *Mahabharata* is ten times longer than the Greek epic poems the *Iliad* and the *Odyssey* combined.

All the proceeds earned from James M. Barrie's book *Peter Pan* were bequeathed to the Great Ormond Street Hospital for Sick Children in London.

The French Academy took 297 years, from 1635 to 1932, to write a grammar book of 263 pages. When finally published, it contained fifty typographical errors.

The hero in Robert Burns's poem "Tam O'Shanter" gave his name to the flat Scottish wool cap with a pompom at its center.

Huckleberry Finn's remedy for warts was swinging a dead cat in a graveyard at night.

More than 63 million *Star Trek* books, in more than

fifteen languages, are in print; thirteen are sold every minute in the United States.

The smallest book in the Library of Congress is *Old King Cole*. It is 1/25 of an inch by 1/25 of an inch. The pages can only be turned with the use of a needle.

The largest book in the Library of Congress is John James Audubon's *Birds of America*, containing life-size illustrations of birds. The book is 39.37 inches high.

There are more than 375 organizations around the world devoted to Sherlock Holmes. The largest group is the Japan Sherlock Holmes Club, with more than twelve hundred members.

In 1955, a book was returned to Cambridge University Library—288 years overdue.

Emily Dickinson wrote more than nine hundred poems, of which only four were published during her lifetime.

Gone with the Wind was the only book written by Margaret Mitchell.

Charles Dickens earned no more money from his many books than he did from doing lectures.

None of Charles Dickens's works have ever gone out of print.

In the 1631 publication of the Bible, a printer accidentally omitted the word "not" from the seventh commandment, encouraging readers to commit adultery.

The very first book about plastic surgery was written in 1597.

There is approximately one library book for each and every person on earth.

Offered a new pen to write with, 97 percent of all people will write their own name.

More books have been written about Jack the Ripper than any other murderer in the world.

Charles Darwin thought that the 1,250-copy first run of his book *The Origin of Species* was too much, but the books sold out the first day of publication.

There have been copies made of the Holy Bible and the Koran that are small enough to fit in a walnut shell.

The first publication of the *Encyclopaedia Britannica* came out in 1768.

Hans Christian Andersen was dyslexic.

Books that are made in the present day only have a life expectancy of about one hundred years because the sulfuric acid in the wood-pulp paper rots rapidly.

There are more than thirteen thousand existing towns and cities in Great Britain that can claim to have been mentioned in the Domesday Book.

Lord Byron, considered one of the most dashing and attractive men of his time, struggled with his weight and had a clubfoot.

John Grisham is a distant cousin of President Bill Clinton.

Several British towns have feuded over which has the right to call itself Jane Austen's real home. Bath, which holds a Jane Austen Festival, claims that it is the Jane Austen capital because the city is featured in several of her novels. However, Chawton, Austen's home from 1809 until her death, contains the cottage where she completed all her novels.

Some Jane Austen fans are so passionate that they want their ashes scattered at the seventeenth-century Hampshire Cottage where she wrote her novels. The management of the museum was forced to issue a statement declaring that while they appreciate the enthusiasm of Austen's fans, they cannot allow ashes to be laid because "it is distressing for visitors to see mounds of human ash, particularly so for our gardener. Also, it is of no benefit to the garden!"

Don Quixote has been translated into more languages than any book apart from the Bible.

Anne of Green Gables is an extremely popular book in Japan even a hundred years after the book was published. There has been a musical, TV series, comic books, and magazines devoted to learning practices depicted in the book, such as quilting, having tea, and developing an appreciation for nature. Visiting Prince Edward Island in Canada, the setting for the novel, has become a Japanese rite of passage. A theme park in Japan called Canadian World, which closed in 1998, included replicas of places from the novel, and a school of social work and nursing on the island of Honshu is called the School of Green Gables.

There really was a Cyrano de Bergerac. He was a fiction writer who lived from about 1619 to 1655, had a big nose, and dueled.

At one time, Chinese books had the footnotes printed at the top of the page.

Two out of every three women in the world are illiterate.

Some publishers claim that science-fiction readers are better educated than the average book buyer.

◊ IT'S ALL BARD

The first person other than royalty to be portrayed on a British stamp was William Shakespeare, in 1964.

There is no living descendant of Shakespeare.

Shakespeare's signature is worth millions of dollars, as there are only six known specimens in the entire world.

In Shakespeare's *Julius Caesar*, there is a reference to a clock striking, but clocks did not appear until at least a thousand years after Caesar's death.

In Shakespeare's *Winter's Tale*, he writes about a ship that has been wrecked off the coast of Bohemia, yet Bohemia has never had a coastline.

WORDY MATTERS

Etymology is the study of the history of words.

Conchology is the study of shells.

Brontology is the study of thunder.

Of all the professionals in the United States, journalists are credited with having the largest vocabulary—approximately twenty thousand words. On average, clergymen, lawyers, and doctors each have fifteen thousand words in their vocabulary. Skilled workers who haven't had a college education know between five thousand and seven thousand words, and farm laborers know about sixteen hundred.

The word "palace" comes from the name of one of the hills in the ancient city of Rome—the Palatine Hill.

The word "education" is based on the Latin *educo*, which means "to draw out."

The word "taxi" is spelled the same in English, German, French, Swedish, and Portuguese.

There are more than forty thousand characters in traditional Chinese script.

Martin K. Tytell, an expert in typewriters, was known as Mr. Typewriter. The post office would deliver to him all letters addressed to "Mr. Typewriter, New York." When he mistakenly inserted a character upside down on a Burmese typewriter, it became a standard, even in Burma.

The phrase "in the limelight" originated from chemist Robert Hare discovering that a blowpipe flame acting upon a block of calcium oxide (lime) produced a brilliant white light that could be used to illuminate theater stages.

A "keeper" is the loop on a belt that holds the loose end.

There are three sets of letters on the standard type-writer and computer keyboards that are in alphabetical order reading left to right. They are F-G-H, J-K-L, and O-P.

A "vamp" is the upper front top of a shoe.

The expression "knuckle down" originated with marbles—players put knuckles to the ground for their best shots.

The expression "nervous Nellie" refers to Frank Kellogg, the secretary of state under Calvin Coolidge, who was put down because he displayed "un-manly" traits like caution and fear. He was also the recipient of a Nobel Peace Prize.

The piece that protrudes from the top end of an umbrella is called a ferrule. The word "ferrule" is also used to describe the piece of metal that holds a rubber eraser on a pencil.

The little bits of paper left over when holes are punched in data cards or tape are called "chads."

Absterse is a little-used verb meaning "to clean."

The most commonly misspelled word in the English language is "supersede" according to a survey quoted in London's *Daily Telegraph*, which suggested that perhaps the root of most common misspellings is simply that some people are too "clever."

In literature, the average length of a sentence is around thirty-five words.

More than a thousand languages are spoken in Africa.

Based on population, Chinese Mandarin is the most commonly spoken language in the world. Spanish follows second, English third, and Bengali fourth.

All pilots on international flights identify themselves in English, regardless of their country of origin.

Natives of the Turkish village of Kuskoy communicate through whistling, which allows them to communicate over distances of up to one mile.

Hundreds of years ago people traveling by stagecoach in Britain often sent a servant ahead to make arrangements for their arrival. The servant would give money "to insure promptness," which was shortened by initials to "tip." Today a tip is more of a thank-you after good service than a bribe to get good service.

Kissing one's fingertips is a common gesture throughout Europe and Latin America countries, declaring "Ah, beautiful!" The gesture originates from the ancient Greeks and Romans, who, when entering and leaving the temple, threw a kiss toward sacred objects such as statues and altars.

READ ALL ABOUT IT

Almost half the newspapers in the world are published in the United States and Canada.

Anyone writing a letter to the *New York Times* has one chance in twenty-one of having the letter published. Letter writers to the *Washington Post* do significantly better, with one letter out of eight finding its way to print.

A Sunday edition of the *New York Times* uses the equivalent of 63,000 trees.

A full-page color ad in *Vogue*, seen by 1.2 million people, costs $80,000.

The first advertisement printed in English in 1477 offered a prayer book. The ad was published by William Caxton on his press in Westminster Abbey. No price was mentioned, only that the book was "good chepe."

The Procrastinators' Club of America sends news to its members under the masthead "Last Month's Newsletter."

The *Washington Daily News* was the first newspaper to use a perfumed advertising page.

> Legend has it that the *Los Angeles Times* used to be so heavy that a paper thrown on the porch of actress Barbara Bain killed her dog. Since then the paper has been much lighter in weight.

The July 21, 2008, edition of New Hampshire and Vermont's *Valley News* featured a surprising typo—the paper misspelled its own name on the front page as "Valley Newss." In a correction the next day the editor said, "Let us say for the record: We sure feel silly."

A Sporting Chance

GAME ON

There are 170,000,000,000,000,000,000,000,000 ways to play the ten opening moves in a game of chess.

> The horizontal lines on a chessboard are called ranks. The vertical lines are called files.

On a bingo card of ninety numbers, there are approximately 44 million ways to make B-I-N-G-O.

> The game of Monopoly is the bestselling board game in the world, licensed or sold in eighty countries and produced in twenty-six languages.

The most landed-on squares in Monopoly are New York Avenue, Illinois Avenue, B&O Railroad, and Reading Railroad.

Dice used in crap games in Las Vegas are manufactured to a tolerance of 0.0002 inches, less than 1/17 the thickness of a human hair, in order to prevent some numbers from occurring more frequently than others.

More cheating takes place in private, friendly gambling games than in all other gambling games combined.

The children's game Rock, Paper, Scissors is also popular in Japan, where it is called Janken. The game is also played by some children using their feet, with closed feet equaling rock (*gu*), spread legs equaling paper (*pa*), and one foot behind the other equaling scissors (*choki*).

The game Scrabble is found in one out of every three American homes.

The highest known score for a single word in competition Scrabble is 392. In 1982, Dr. Saladin Khoshnaw achieved this score for the word "caziques," which means "Indian chiefs."

The first set of ice hockey rules were drawn up in 1865.

A rubber cube was originally used instead of a ball in hockey.

The original basket in basketball, as invented by James Naismith in 1891, was a peach basket.

Football player Eli Manning once reprogrammed a teammate's cell phone so all its displays would be in Japanese, and replaced all his offensive linemen's shoes with purple ones.

Octupush is an underwater hockey game played between teams.

Amateur baseball players are called "sandlotters."

The line from behind which darts are thrown is called the "hockey."

Two is the lowest possible score to conclude a game of darts.

Yorker, googly, and chinaman are styles of bowling in cricket.

A badminton racquet was once known as a battledore.

Dutch and German immigrants introduced ninepin bowling to the United States.

MAMA SAID KNOCK YOU OUT

Escrima is a Philippine martial art using sticks, knives, and hands.

In Japan, the deadly martial art called *tessenjutsu* is based solely on the use of a fan.

More than 80 percent of professional boxers have suffered brain damage.

Boxer Sugar Ray Leonard won titles at five different weights.

Rocky Marciano is the only world heavyweight boxing champion to remain undefeated throughout his entire professional career.

SOCCER IT TO ME

FIFA referee Ken Aston thought up the idea of red and yellow cards.

The Azteca, Etrusco Unico, Questra, and Tricolore were all types of soccer balls used for World Cup Final tournaments.

The original FA Cup was stolen in 1895 and never recovered.

Singapore hosted a RoboCup in 1998, involving teams of robot soccer players.

Only eight players have scored a total of ten or more goals in World Cup Finals tournaments.

THE RUNDOWN

The Nike "swoosh" logo was designed by University of Oregon student Carolyn Davidson in 1964, and she was initially paid $35 dollars for her design.

Olympic double-winning marathon runner Abebe Bikila won one race barefoot, the other in shoes.

The Boston Marathon is the world's oldest annual race, starting in 1897.

British father and son Donald and Michael Campbell both held the land speed record.

I WOULD WALK 500 MILES . . .

In 1909 Edward Payson Weston walked 3,795 miles, from New York to San Francisco, in 104 days and 7 hours to celebrate his seventieth birthday. The following year he walked back to New York from Los Angeles. He completed the 3,600-mile trek in 76 days and 23 hours.

TENNIS, ANYONE?

Full seeding at Wimbledon began in 1927.

From 1985 to 1991 Boris Becker only once failed to appear in the Wimbledon men's singles final, in 1987.

When the first tennis racquets appeared in the 1920s the strings were made from piano wire.

The Virginia Slims tennis championship is the only tournament where women play the best of five sets.

RACING STRIPES

Between one and two jockeys are killed each year while horse-racing.

Horse-racing regulations state that no racehorse's name may contain more than eighteen letters. Names that are too long would be cumbersome on racing sheets.

Sumner, Bramich, and McKee are all types of hares used in greyhound racing.

Breeders Cup Day is the richest day's sport in the world.

One Formula 1 tire costs approximately $1,200.

The first Grand Prix World Championship was held in 1950.

PAR FOR THE COURSE

Eight competitors took part in the 1860 British Golf Open.

The two courses at Emirates Golf Club in Dubai need 2 million gallons of water each day during the summer to keep them in condition.

A fan at the 1999 Phoenix Golf Open was arrested for carrying a gun.

OLYMPIC FEVER

The ancient Olympic Games started in 776 BCE. They ended in 395 BCE when Olympia was destroyed by an earthquake.

Men's basketball was officially added to the Olympic Games program at the 1936 Summer Olympics in Berlin.

Synchronized swimming was introduced to the Olympics in 1984.

At the time swimmer Michael Phelps won his record-breaking eighth gold medal at the 2008 Olympics, he would have been fourth in the gold medal count (if he were his own country) after China, the United States, and Germany, and tied with Australia.

After gymnast Shawn Johnson won gold in the balance beam at the 2008 Olympics, she was honored at the Iowa State Fair with a likeness of her carved in butter. She joins such luminaries as Elvis, John Wayne, and Harry Potter in the State Fair's pantheon of butter honorees.

In 2000, Olympic racewalker Jane Saville was disqualified on her way back into the stadium. Afterward, when asked what she needed, she tearfully replied, "A gun to shoot myself."

During the women's 20k racewalk at the 2008 Olympics, one announcer said of the leader, "She's walking away with this one!"

Chinese officials were so worried about appearing hospitable to foreign visitors during the 2008 games in Beijing they distributed posters around the city with helpful instructions on interacting with foreigners. Among the recommendations: Don't ask about income, expenses, age, love life, health, name or address, personal experiences, religious belief, political views, or occupation. When interacting with handicapped athletes, use polite forms of address and avoid using platitudes or insulting phrases such as telling a blind person "It's over there." When walking with foreigners, men should help women carry things, but not their handbags.

FOOD FOR THOUGHT

BEVERAGE SERVICE

In 1938, a comic strip titled "Pepsi and Pete" was used to advertise Pepsi-Cola.

The lion used with the slogan "King of Beverages" constituted an early Dr Pepper ad campaign.

Tea bags were invented as early as 1903 and were first successfully marketed by New York tea and coffee shop merchant Thomas Sullivan. The first tea bags were hand-sewn.

One pound of tea can make nearly three hundred cups.

The drink Ovaltine was originally named Ovomaltine, but a clerical error changed it when the manufacturer registered the name.

The first bottles of Coca-Cola were sold in 1894. Coke was not sold in a can until 1955.

The word "whiskey" comes from the Gaelic *uisge beatha*, meaning "water of life." Any whiskey distilled in Scotland is called Scotch whisky and is often referred to simply as "Scotch" in other countries, while in the United States all other types are spelled "whiskey."

People in Siberia often buy milk frozen on a stick. Milk is technically considered to be a food and not a beverage. Containing almost 250 chemical compounds, it is the most complex food on earth.

There is more alcohol in mouthwash than in wine.

Alcoholics are twice as likely to confess a drinking problem to a computer as they are to confess to a doctor.

In Poland, a brewery once developed a plumbing problem in which beer was accidentally pumped into the incoming water supply. It meant that residents of the town got free beer on tap for one day.

An Irish woman traveled to Finland to find a "husband" to carry her over a 253-meter track to win her weight (264 pounds) in beer. The contest is said to stem from a nineteenth-century legend in which a notorious thief, Ronkainen the Robber, made wannabe members of his posse carry grain or swine along a course. Others claim that the contest stems from the ancient practice of wife-stealing.

Bottled water costs between 250 and 10,000 times more than tap water, but in blind taste testing people usually can't tell the difference.

In 2000 an executive told a group of Wall Street analysts that tap water would eventually be used only for showers and washing dishes.

In 2002 Nestlé produced a training manual for waiters called Pour on the Tips. Converting guests to bottled water instead of tap, it said, could boost their monthly earnings by a hundred dollars or more.

GROUNDS FOR DISCUSSION

The first coffeehouse in New York opened in Manhattan in 1696.

The world's most expensive coffee, at $130 a pound, is called Kopi Luwak. It is in the droppings of a type of marsupial that eats only the very best coffee beans. Plantation workers track them and scoop their precious excrement.

Large doses of coffee can be lethal. Ten grams, or one hundred cups over four hours, can kill the average human.

The coffee served at gourmet coffee shops like Starbucks has 50 percent more caffeine than regular drip coffee.

Centuries ago, men were told that the evil effects of coffee would make them sterile; women were cautioned to avoid caffeine unless they wanted to be barren.

It typically takes five or six cycles of two to four hours to flush caffeine completely out of the system. Women and smokers metabolize caffeine more quickly than men and nonsmokers; Asians metabolize it the slowest.

Of devout coffee drinkers, about 62 percent of those who are thirty-five to forty-nine years of age say they become upset if they don't have a cup of coffee at their regular time. Only 50 percent of those under age thirty-five become upset.

New studies are constantly touting the surprising benefits of caffeine and coffee. For instance: Caffeine may help prevent autoimmune diseases such as multiple sclerosis and relieves asthma symptoms. Drinking moderate amounts of coffee is believed to slash rates of Parkinson's disease, inhibit the formation of gallstones, ward off cirrhosis, and may even help prevent Alzheimer's. One study also showed that a person's suicide risk decreased with each cup of coffee consumed per day, up to seven cups. However, eight cups or more was shown in a separate study to *increase* the risk substantially.

A serving of coffee has more antioxidants than a serving of either grape juice or blueberries.

HOW SWEET IT IS

Per capita, the Irish eat more chocolate than Americans, Swedes, Danes, French, or Italians.

Licorice can raise blood pressure.

Lime Jell-O gives off the same brain waves as adult humans when hooked up to an EEG machine.

From 1941 until 1950, violet was part of the color mixture for M&M's plain chocolates, but it was replaced by tan.

Film critic Roger Ebert once received a letter from a man claiming to be conducting tests to determine the strength and robustness of M&M's by holding "duels" to see which of them would break first. He found that generally the brown and red ones were tougher, while the blue ones were the weakest. He sent the winning M&M's piece from each pack to the company with a request that they use it "for breeding purposes." The company responded with a coupon for a free half-pound bag of plain M&M's.

A portrait of rapper Eminem was once created out of more than a thousand M&M's candies, and was purchased by Ripley's for inclusion in one of their museums. Oddly, the artist did not use any green M&M's in the work.

Chocolate manufacturers use 40 percent of the world's almonds and 20 percent of the world's peanuts.

"Grunt" and "slump" are two names that refer to a fruit dessert with a biscuit topping.

In the Middle Ages, sugar was a treasured luxury, costing nine times as much as milk.

The dessert parfait's name comes from the French word for "perfect."

The carob can be used to replace chocolate, and often sugar, in cooking.

There are eighteen different animal shapes in the Animal Crackers cookie zoo.

A study once found that when asked to write an essay on either death or a trip to the dentist, people writing about death ate more cookies than those writing about the dentist.

In early 1999, General Mills launched an "Around the World Event" promotion with internationally known marshmallow shapes in its Lucky Charms cereal. These shapes included a purple Liberty Bell, a pink-and-white Leaning Tower of Pisa, a green-and-yellow Statue of Liberty torch, a gold Great Pyramid, a blue Eiffel Tower, an orange Golden Gate

Bridge, a green-and-white Alps, and a red-and-white Big Ben clock.

There is a wild edible plant called Hernandulcin that is a thousand times sweeter than sugar.

McDonald's and Burger King sugarcoat their fries so they will turn golden brown.

The Stay-Puft Marshmallow Man at the end of *Ghostbusters* was 116 feet 6 inches tall.

As the official taste-tester for Edy's Grand Ice Cream, John Harrison had his taste buds insured for $1 million.

July was designated as National Ice Cream Month by Ronald Reagan in 1984. The third Sunday of the month was designated National Ice Cream Day. The agriculture committee that sponsored the bill wrote that it was "sharply divided over the comparative merits of vanilla, chocolate, strawberry, and other flavors, but united in solid bipartisan appreciation of ice cream."

The first soft-serve ice cream maker was either J. F. McCullough or Tom Carvel. McCullough first offered his soft serve to customers at a friend's ice cream shop in Kankakee, Illinois, in 1938, and 1,600 people paid 10 cents for all they could eat. Two years later, McCullough and his son teamed up with Harry Oltz, who had invented a machine that could produce a continuous flow of the frozen mixture, to open the first Dairy Queen, in Joliet, Illinois. Carvel appears to have discovered soft serve about the same time. When his truck carrying ice cream broke down, he sold it from the truck over two days as it softened.

When Toll House Inn owner Ruth Wakefield invented the chocolate chip cookie either by accident or in a moment of inspiration to improve the taste of her Butter Drop Do cookies (legend has it a bar of chocolate fell into the industrial mixer), she sold the Toll House brand and recipe to Nestlé in return for a lifetime supply of chocolate. However, a crucial step to the recipe is to chill the dough overnight, a fact that Nestlé left out of the version of the recipe that is printed on its packages of chocolate.

DESTINATION CUISINE

In an authentic Chinese meal, the last course is soup because it allows the roast duck entrée to "swim" toward digestion.

The largest item on any menu in the world is roast camel, sometimes served at Bedouin wedding feasts. The camel is stuffed with a sheep's carcass, which is stuffed with chickens, which are stuffed with fish, which are stuffed with eggs.

Okonomiyaki is considered to be Japan's answer to pizza.

It consists of a potpourri of grilled vegetables, noodles, and meat or seafood, placed between two pancakelike layers of fried batter.

In Japan, some restaurants serve smaller portions to women, even though the charge is the same as a man's portion.

Spain produces more olive oil than Italy does.

"Poached egg" means "egg in a bag" from the French word *poche*. When an egg is poached, the white of the egg forms a pocket around the yolk, hence the name.

"Sherbet" is Australian slang for beer.

On the Italian Riviera in Viareggio, there is a culinary tradition that a good soup must always contain one stone from the sea.

In a traditional French restaurant kitchen, a *garde manger* is the person responsible for the preparation and presentation of cold foods.

Mouse flesh was once considered a great delicacy in ancient China and certain parts of India. In ancient Greece, mice were sometimes devoured by temple priests, as the mouse was sacred to Apollo.

In ancient Rome, it was considered a sin to eat the flesh of a woodpecker, and oysters were so highly prized that they were sold for their weight in gold.

In the early American Indians of the southwestern United States only ate the organs of the animals they hunted for food, and left the muscles for predatory animals. Their meat-eating habits were changed by European influences.

The ancient Greeks considered parsley too sacred to eat, while Romans served it as a garnish and to improve the taste of food. They believed it had special powers and would keep them sober.

In the Middle East, and later in Europe, doctors blamed the eggplant for all sorts of things, from epilepsy to cancer. In the fifth century, Chinese women made a black dye from eggplant skins to stain and polish their teeth, while some people in medieval Europe considered the eggplant an aphrodisiac.

The Egyptians ate mustard by tossing the seeds into their mouths while chewing meat.

As late as 1720 in America, eating potatoes was believed to shorten a person's life.

Only men were allowed to eat at the first self-service restaurant, the Exchange Buffet, in New York in 1885.

Grasshoppers are the most popular insect snack in some parts of the world.

Port Alba, the first known pizza shop, opened in 1830 in Naples and is still open today.

About 27 percent of food in developed countries is wasted each year, being simply thrown away.

The turnip originated in Greece.

Tibetans drink tea made of salt and rancid yak butter.

The average French citizen eats five hundred snails a year.

Chicken soup was believed to be an aphrodisiac in the Middle Ages.

Since Hindus don't eat beef, the McDonald's in New Delhi makes its burgers with mutton.

In ancient times, parsley wreaths were used to ward off drunkenness.

Cheese is the oldest of all man-made foods. The United States is the leading producer of cheese, at 6.8 billion pounds per year. France is the leading consumer of cheese, at 43.6 pounds per person per year.

SEA-SONAL DELIGHTS

One of the fattiest fishes is salmon; four ounces of the fish contains nine grams of fat.

Oysters were a major part of life in New York in the late 1800s as oystering supported a large number of families. They were prepared in various ways and eaten for breakfast, lunch, and dinner.

Young oysters in France have been plagued by outbreaks of oyster herpes virus type 1, which scientists say is triggered when baby oysters expend too much energy developing their sexual organs instead of their natural defenses.

The custom of serving a slice of lemon with fish dates back to the Middle Ages. It was believed that if a person accidentally swallowed a fish bone, the lemon juice would dissolve it.

Japan is the largest harvester of seafood in the world, taking 15 percent of the world's total catch.

The average Iceland resident eats nearly two hundred pounds of fish every year.

TODAY'S MENU

About 800 million people in the world are malnourished.

Four percent of the food people eat in a lifetime is consumed in front of an open refrigerator.

There are more than thirty thousand diets on public record.

Of about 350 million cans of chicken noodle soup, of all commercial brands sold annually in the United States, 60 percent are purchased during the cold and flu season. January is the top-selling month of the year.

In 1996, Gerber introduced chicken alfredo as one of its new flavors of baby food.

The can opener was invented forty-eight years after cans were introduced.

There is no fat in ketchup.

Peanut oil is used for underwater cooking in submarines. Undersea fleets like it because it does not smoke unless heated above 450°F.

Nachos were first brought to Los Angeles by a waitress

named Carmen Rocha in 1959. She brought the recipe with her from San Antonio, Texas, where she'd learned how to layer tortilla wedges with shredded cheddar cheese and slices of jalapeño pepper.

A woman in California founded a nonprofit organization that gives piglets to Nepalese families in exchange for promises that their daughters will be sent to school instead of being sold into slavery. The grown pigs fetch about thirty-five to seventy-five dollars, which is the same amount buyers would pay for a girl. Already, this switcheroo has saved three thousand girls.

BRAND LOYALTY

French's mustard, which was never French (it was created as a salad topping by American brothers named French for the 1904 St. Louis World's Fair) is now owned by a British conglomerate.

The Midwestern chain Caribou Coffee was dreamed up by a Minneapolis couple on their honeymoon trip out west. They eventually sold out to the Islamic venture capital firm Arcapita. Arcapita, which conforms to Islamic religious law, also owns fast-food chain Church's Chicken and removed bacon from the menu, pork not being halal.

The original Trader Joe was twenty-six-year-old Joe Coulombe, a manager at Rexall Drug. Joe bought the convenience store chain from Rexall, changed the name, and concentrated on offering affordable, exotic foods with a healthy and environmental bent. Two German investors bought Coulombe out in 1979 but kept him as CEO.

The Southland Ice Company started selling food at off hours to customers in 1927 but didn't change its name to 7-Eleven until 1946. A Japanese corporation now owns 7-Eleven.

PRODUCE PARADISE

The pumpkin has been known to develop roots with a total length of 82,000 feet, or more than fifteen miles.

"Baby-cut" carrots aren't really baby carrots. They're actually full-size carrots peeled and ground down to size.

Once an orange is squeezed or cut, the vitamin C dissipates quickly. After only eight hours at room temperature or a scant twenty-four hours in the refrigerator, there is a 20 percent vitamin C loss.

A potato has no more calories than an apple.

The darker an olive is, the higher the oil content.

Peas will lose their bright green color if cooked in a

covered pot with acidic ingredients, such as lemon juice, wine, or tomatoes.

Paper can be made from asparagus.

Pears ripen better off the tree, and they ripen from the inside out.

Onions, apples, and potatoes all have the same taste; their smell causes the perceived differences in flavor.

Using two forks and a charge will cause a pickle to emit light.

Tomatoes with a strawberry inside have been successfully grown.

The boysenberry is a mixture of the Pacific blackberry, the loganberry, and the raspberry.

The globe artichoke belongs to the daisy family.

Corn is the only cereal crop with American origins.

The world's deadliest mushroom is the *Amanita phalloides*, the death cap.

The strawberry is the only agricultural product that bears its seeds on the outside.

Watermelons can have a Viagra-like effect on the body and may increase libido. Citrulline, a phytonutriant that occurs in watermelons, has the ability to relax blood vessels.

> People who eat fresh fruit daily have 24 percent fewer heart attacks and 32 percent fewer strokes than those who don't.

NUT CASE

Pecan crops need a freeze to help loosen the nuts from their shells.

> The United States produces more than 80 percent of the world's pecans. Georgia, New Mexico, Arizona, and Oklahoma are the states with the top production rates.

The cashew nut, in its natural state, contains poisonous oil. Roasting removes the oil and makes the nuts safe to eat.

More than 45,000 pieces of plastic debris float on every square mile of ocean.

Urine was once used as a detergent for washing.

An average toilet uses three gallons of water every time it is flushed.

Pocket calculators first appeared in the 1970s.

☙ COMPUTER CONNECTIONS

RAM stands for random-access memory.

IBM is nicknamed "Big Blue."

Laptop computers are around 30 percent more likely to fail than a computer that stays in one place.

About 35 percent of companies have bought the Internet domain name for their brand followed by the word "sucks," as well as other derogatory phrases, to avoid anyone else starting a negative site about them. Xerox owns XeroxStinks.com and IHateXerox.org. Dell could buy DellIsEvil.com, but apparently isn't concerned.

TREE TALES

Japanese cedars have blue-green leaves in summer that turn bronze during the winter months.

Science Fair

HOUSEHOLD ITEMS

An energy-saving washing machine can save enough money to buy laundry detergent for six months.

The compact disc was invented in 1965.

The first refrigeration device was made in 1748. The first air conditioner was made in 1902.

The minimum safe distance between a wood-burning stove and flammable objects is three feet.

The average lead pencil will draw a line thirty-five miles long or write approximately fifty thousand English words.

Edwin Beard Budding invented the lawn mower in 1830.

Stitching through a piece of sandpaper is an effective way to sharpen a sewing machine needle.

The cedar is the national tree of Lebanon.

The leaves of an oak tree can give off forty thousand gallons of moisture each year.

Avocado trees have collapsed under the weight of their fruit.

The Romans allegedly bought the sycamore tree to Britain.

Forest fires move faster uphill than downhill.

One cord of wood can produce 7.5 million toothpicks.

China uses 45 billion chopsticks per year, using 25 million trees to make them.

Throughout the South Pacific, no building is taller than the tallest palm tree.

FOLIAGE FACTS

The kowhai is the national flower of New Zealand.

Lavender takes it name from the Latin *lavare*, meaning "to wash," because of its use in toilet preparations.

Water lilies were a symbol of immortality in ancient times.

Of the 15,000-odd known species of orchids in the world, 3,000 of them can be found in Brazil.

Bamboo can grow by the height of a two-year-old child a day—three to four feet in a day.

The kerosene fungus can live in jet fuel tanks; the fungus can use the fuel as food.

THE WEATHER REPORT

Approximately 10 billion mathematical calculations are needed for a one-day weather forecast.

The average raindrop falls at fifteen miles per hour.

Dirty snow melts faster than white snow because it reflects less light.

Men are more likely than women to die in floods, partly because they are often outside for their jobs and because they are more likely to take risks in bad weather. Lightning is also another very common fatal disaster for men, supposedly because they are often outside playing or watching sports.

Two hundred and thirty people died when Moradabad, India, was bombed with giant balls of hail more than two inches in diameter.

During medieval times, church bells were often consecrated to ward off evil spirits. The bells would be rung in an attempt to stop thunderstorms, which were believed to be the work of demons.

LIGHTNING STRIKES

An average lightning bolt generates temperatures five times hotter than those found at the sun's surface.

A typical lightning bolt is only one inch wide and five miles long.

The longest lightning bolt recorded was 118 miles long.

Lightning bolts can generate up to 200 million volts of electricity.

There are more than 16 million lightning storms every year.

Lightning is more likely than not to strike twice in the same place. Like all electric currents or discharges, lightning follows the path of least resistance.

In Britain, two women were killed in 1999 by lightning conducted through their underwire bras.

A church steeple in Germany was struck by lightning and destroyed on April 18, 1599. The members of the church rebuilt it, but it was hit by lightning three more times between then and 1783, and rebuilt again and again. Every time it was hit, the date was April 18.

I FEEL THE EARTH MOVE

The 1906 San Francisco earthquake was the energy-output equivalent of twelve thousand Hiroshima nuclear bombs.

Tangshan, China, suffered the deadliest earthquake of the twentieth century on July 28, 1976. The quake registered at 7.8 on the Richter scale and killed or seriously injured one-quarter of the population.

Major earthquakes have hit Japan on September 1, 827; September 1, 859; September 1, 1185; September 1, 1649; and September 1, 1923.

WATER WONDERS

A mile on the ocean and a mile on land are not the same distance. On the ocean, a nautical mile measures 6,076 feet, while a land mile is 5,278 feet.

It has been estimated that the deep seas may contain as many as 10 million species that have yet to be discovered.

In the past ten years, more than fifteen hundred new species have been discovered in Australian waters.

Assuming a rate of one drop per second, a leaking tap wastes about seven thousand liters of water in a year.

The hardness of ice is similar to that of concrete.

If hot water is suddenly poured into a glass, that glass is more likely to break if it is thick than if it is thin. Hence, test tubes are made of thin glass.

It takes as much heat to turn one ounce of snow to water as it does to make one ounce of soup boil at room temperature.

SPACE CASE

Halley's Comet will next appear in 2061.

Two objects have struck the earth, specifically Siberia, with enough force to destroy a whole city. Not one human being was hurt either time. The 1996 *Guinness Book of World Records* stated that due to the rotation of the Earth, if the 1908 collision (in which the meteor actually exploded before hitting the Earth's surface) had occurred four hours and forty-seven minutes later, it would have completely destroyed the city of Saint Petersburg.

The only reported animal fatality from meteorite impacts is an Egyptian dog that was killed in 1911 by the Nakhla meteorite, although this report is disputed.

The first known modern case of a human hit by a space rock occurred on November 30, 1954, in

Sylacauga, Alabama, when a stone chondrite crashed through a roof and hit Ann Hodges in her living room after it bounced off her radio. She was badly bruised.

The sun is estimated to be twenty to twenty-one cosmic years old. One cosmic year is equal to 225 million Earth years.

The sun's warming rays travel 93 million miles to reach Earth.

It would take a car traveling at one hundred miles per hour nearly 30 million years to reach our nearest star.

The number of stars in the galaxy is now less than the national deficit.

A manned rocket reaches the moon in less time than it took a stagecoach to travel the length of Britain.

The former planet Pluto was named by eleven-year-old schoolgirl Venetia Phair in 1930 when her grandfather passed on her suggestion to astronomers. Her grandfather gave her a five-pound note for her contribution.

In 2008 Pluto was demoted from being a planet to a new designation: a plutoid.

The word of the year for 2006 from the American Dialect Society was "plutoed," meaning "demoted."

The Kuiper Belt object Makemake is one of the first space rocks to receive the new designation of planetoid or plutoid from the International Astronomical Union.

☙ EARTHBOUND

It would take eighty moons to equal the weight of the Earth.

If all the heat emanating from the Earth's internal sources could be converted into electricity, it would result in enough power to equal three times the global human energy consumption.

If you were to dig a hole from one side of the Earth to the other and jump into it, it would take about forty-two minutes to reach the opposite end. At that point you would fall back into the hole and repeat the trip back and forth forever.

It takes the same amount of time to fall all the way through the Earth and back as it does to orbit it, if orbiting right at the Earth's surface.

The Earth would be smoother than the surface of a billiard ball if it were shrunk to that size.

The Earth gains about twenty to forty tons of weight each

day due to meteors and other space debris landing on the surface. At that rate it would take 450,000 trillion years to double the mass of the planet.

ELEMENTAL EQUATIONS

Helium is the element with the lowest boiling point.

An ounce of platinum can be stretched to ten thousand feet.

A quality, round brilliant diamond has at least fifty-eight facets.

Only one in a thousand polished diamonds weighs more than a carat.

Glass can be made so strong that a pressure of 350 tons is required to crush a two-inch cube, and it can be made so fragile that breath will break a drinking glass.

It takes ten tons of ore to produce one ounce of platinum.

Granite conducts sound ten times faster than air.

If all the gold suspended in the world's seawater were mined, each person on earth would receive about nine pounds.

DEPARTMENT OF
MOTOR VEHICLES

Wheeled vehicles were first invented around 3000 BCE.

The average car uses 1.6 ounces of gas idling for one minute, while .5 ounces is used to start the vehicle.

The name of the statuette atop the hood of every Rolls-Royce car is the Spirit of Ecstasy.

In 2007, Americans consumed more than 868 million gallons of petroleum per day.

In a survey, 605 motorists said they sometimes leave their keys in the ignition of their unattended car.

There are no rental cars in Bermuda.

Canada is the largest importer of American cars.

On average, fifty-one cars a year overshoot and drive into the canals of Amsterdam.

In China there are six hundred bicycles for every car.

In Tokyo, a bicycle is faster than a car for most trips of less than fifty minutes.

The Netherlands is credited with having the most bikes in the world. One bike per person is the national average, with an estimated 16 million bicycles nationwide.

The Indiana Toll Road links the Midwest to the East Coast. The state of Indiana built the road in 1965 and then leased it to a joint venture of Spanish and Australian companies for $3.8 billion in 2006 for seventy-five years. The Chicago Skyway was leased by the same consortium for $1.83 billion for a ninety-nine-year lease starting in 2005.

MECHANICAL MARVELS

The first women flight attendants, in 1930, were required to be single, trained nurses between twenty and twenty-six years of age, no more than five feet four inches tall and 118 pounds.

Fifty percent of the adult Dutch population has never flown in a plane, and 28 percent admit a fear of flying.

The tallest and fastest roller coaster in the world is the 456-foot-tall Kingda Ka of Six Flags Great Adventure in New Jersey. The roller coaster reaches speeds of 128 miles per hour.

The world's longest escalator is in Ocean Park, Hong Kong. With a length of 745 feet, the escalator boasts a vertical rise of 377 feet.

A STITCH IN TIME

An English builder named William Willett, and not Benjamin Franklin as is often believed, was the inventor of daylight saving time (DST), among other reasons because he disliked cutting short his round of golf at dusk. He proposed it in 1907 but died before it was enacted into law. He is also the great-great-grandfather of Coldplay lead singer Chris Martin.

DST reduces traffic fatalities because of the extra afternoon daylight.

Changes in DST have a significant economic effect, once supposedly costing U.S. stock exchanges a one-day loss of $31 billion.

Idaho senators once supported an extension of DST on the basis that fast-food restaurants would then sell more french fries made with Idaho potatoes.

Southern Brazil observes DST; equatorial Brazil does not. Most countries near the equator do not observe it because sunrise times do not vary enough to necessitate it.

Iraq observed DST from 2003 to 2007, but did not observe it in 2008.

In 1999, Palestinian terrorists transporting a bomb that

they thought was set to go off at 5:30 p.m. Israel standard time were killed when the bomb exploded early; it was actually set for 5:30 p.m. Palestinian daylight time, which was an hour ahead.

Most of the world does not observe DST, because much of Africa and Asia does not observe it.

Hawaii does not observe DST except for three weeks in 1933. There is no record as to why it was implemented or discontinued.

Greenwich mean time was established in 1635 to help mariners determine longitude at sea. Britain did not establish it as the legal time until 1880, even though most clocks by then had been using it for decades.

China, despite its large size, uses only a single time zone.

Any calendar date exists in some place on the globe for fifty hours due to the twenty-six-hour gap between the earliest and latest time zones.

Three time zones meet at the borders of Finland, Norway, and Russia.

At the 2008 Beijing Olympics a sign next to the clock in the *New York Times* press center read: "This clock is Beijing time. If you need to know the time in New

York, check the clock on the wall at the opposite end of the room." The clock at the other end of the room showed the exact same time, since New York time is exactly twelve hours behind Beijing time on standard (not military or twenty-four-hour) clocks.

THE HUMAN BODY

THE EARLY YEARS

A human fetus acquires fingerprints at the age of three months.

The weight of a fetus increases by about 2.4 billion times in nine months.

Some babies suck their thumb before they are born.

As babies develop in the uterus, their bodies are covered in fine, downy hair called lanugo, which usually disappears before they are born.

Children born in the month of May are, on average, seven ounces heavier at birth than children born in any other month.

Babies are born with the ability to swim and hold their breath, but they quickly lose this instinct.

All humans are born with the reflexes for shivering, urinating, and the knee-jerk reaction when the tendon below the knee is tapped.

Newborn babies can discriminate between degrees of brightness and have approximately 20/20 vision. They are not blind.

Most newborns cry without tears until they are three to six weeks old.

Babies' strongest sense is smell.

Unlike adults, children can breathe and swallow at the same time until they are seven months old.

Babies like pretty faces better than plain ones.

In toddlers, 29 percent of non-food-related choking accidents are caused by balloons and 19 percent by balls and marbles. Older children are more likely to die from balloons than are toddlers.

Six-year-olds laugh an average of three hundred times a day. Adults only laugh fifteen to one hundred times a day.

The common cold will delay a child's growth for the duration of the cold.

Between 10 and 30 percent of all children have one or more sleepwalking episodes between the ages of seven and twelve.

Some babies, especially those with low birth weight, stop breathing for very brief periods during sleep.

Twins are born less frequently in the eastern part of the world than in the western part.

UNDER SIEGE

More than 1.5 million people die from malaria every year.

There are more bacteria in the mouth than there are people in the world.

The average human body holds enough sulfur to kill all the fleas on a dog, enough potassium to fire a toy cannon, enough carbon to make 900 pencils, enough fat to make seven bars of soap, and enough phosphorus to make 2,200 match heads.

The Spanish flu was unlike most flu viruses, as it hit the young and healthy hardest. The pandemic killed anywhere from 20 million to 100 million people worldwide. To compare: half as many people died in World War I.

There are more than one hundred different viruses that cause the common cold.

Some plastic surgeons now require their prospective patients to complete a psychological evaluation to determine if they can become emotionally unstable or threatening to the doctor after their cosmetic surgery.

Up to 2 million people are hospitalized and as many as 140,000 die each year from reactions to prescription drugs.

In ancient Rome, gold salves were used for the treatment of skin ulcers. Today, gold leaf plays an important role in the treatment of chronic ulcers.

In medieval Europe, alchemists mixed powdered gold into drinks to "comfort sore limbs," one of the earliest references to arthritis.

During the late eighteenth century, Prussian surgeons treated people who stuttered by snipping off portions of their tongues.

Ninety-eight percent of all acute sunstroke cases are fatal.

Pain travels at a speed of 350 feet per second.

FLEXING SOME MUSCLE

The average male adult, having about seventy to eighty pounds of muscle, can bench-press 88 percent of his body weight.

> The average man's muscles comprise about 40 percent of his body weight, or about seventy pounds. In comparison, the average woman's muscles make up about 30 percent of her body weight, or about forty-three pounds.

According to a report in *Dentistry*, scientists have estimated that speech involves at least one hundred muscles. In normal speaking, humans make about fourteen sounds per second. Therefore, when speaking, people generate fourteen hundred neuromuscular events per second.

> It takes seventeen facial muscles to smile, but forty-two to frown.

Muscles can shorten themselves but cannot lengthen themselves. Every time a muscle contracts, it must be pulled back to its original length by another muscle shortening itself in the other direction.

BONEHEADED

The adult human skull comprises twenty-two bones. An adult human head weighs about eight pounds, or the same as a light bowling ball.

The strongest bone in the body, the thigh bone, is hollow. Ounce for ounce, it has a greater pressure tolerance and bearing strength than a rod of equivalent size in cast steel.

Of the 206 bones in the adult human body, 106 are found in the hands and feet (54 are in the hands, 52 are in the feet).

Human bones can withstand being squeezed twice as hard as granite. Bones can also stand being stretched four times as much as concrete.

Human bones can withstand stresses of 24,000 pounds per square inch.

An astronaut's bones lose a measurable amount of weight and thickness after being in space for a prolonged period of time.

From birth to adolescence, selected bones in the human body fuse together. The last bone to fuse is the clavicle, or the collarbone.

Humans have several vestigial anatomical characteristics, including the remnants of a tail (the tailbone).

The human spinal cord reaches its full length by the time a person is four or five years old.

◧ A LEG UP

Most people's legs are slightly different lengths.

The knee is the largest and most easily injured of all the joints in the body and the most frequently injured joint, according to the American Academy of Orthopedic Surgeons.

Anthropologists use a standard height of four feet eleven inches to determine if a group of people are pygmies.

The average woman's thighs are one-and-a-half times larger in circumference than the average man's.

SKIN CONDITIONS

The average person sheds about one and a half pounds of skin each year.

The average person's total skin covering would weigh about six pounds if collected in one mass.

If the skin of a 150-pound person were spread out flat, it would cover approximately twenty square feet.

A human can detect the wing of a bee falling on his or her cheek from a height of one centimeter.

The skin is only about as deep as the tip of a ballpoint pen.

One brow wrinkle is the result of 200,000 frowns.

There are about 2 million sweat glands in the average human body.

The average adult loses 540 calories with every quart of sweat. Men sweat about 40 percent more than women.

An average man, on an average day, excretes three quarts of sweat.

Sweat itself is odorless. Only when combined with bacteria that are breaking down dead skin cells does it smell. Smelly sweat is called bromhidrosis. Sweat is composed of water, sodium chloride, potassium salts, urea, and lactic acid.

The palms of the hands and soles of the feet contain more sweat glands than any other part of the body.

The bacteria found on human skin are roughly the numerical equivalent of all the humans on earth.

First-degree burns affect only the very top layers of the skin. Second-degree burns penetrate midway through the skin's thickness. Third-degree burns penetrate and damage the entire thickness of the skin.

Only about 30 percent of teenage males consistently apply sunscreen compared with 46 percent of female teens.

MOUTHING OFF

The average lifespan of a human taste bud is seven to ten days.

The average person has about ten thousand taste buds. Some are on the tongue, but others are under the tongue, on the inside of the cheeks, on the roof of the mouth, and some can even be found on the lips, which are extremely sensitive to salt.

The human tongue registers bitter tastes ten thousand times more strongly than sweet tastes.

A human tongue tastes bitterness toward the back. Salty flavors are detected at the middle of the tongue, and sweet flavors are noticeable at the tip.

Humans, if they are very sensitive to taste, can detect sweetness in a solution of one part sugar to two hundred parts water.

Humans don't actually taste water; they detect the *flavor* of the water.

Right-handed people tend to chew food on the right side of the mouth, and vice versa.

Sixty percent of men spit in public.

At Tokyo's Keio University Hospital, 30 percent of the outpatients diagnosed with throat polyps attributed the cause of the affliction to singing karaoke.

SHOW SOME TEETH

If one identical twin grows up without a given tooth coming in, the second identical twin will usually also grow up without the tooth.

Sometimes a baby is born with one or two of its first teeth already present.

The average American adult male brushes his teeth 1.9 times a day.

Tooth enamel is the hardest substance manufactured by the human body.

Ancient Romans at one time used human urine as an ingredient in their toothpaste.

BRAIN WAVES

Although the average brain comprises 2 percent of a person's total body weight, it requires 25 percent of all oxygen used by the body.

In one day, the human brain generates more electrical impulses than all the telephones in the world put together. These nerve impulses can travel up to 170 miles per hour.

The human three-pound brain is the most complex and orderly arrangement of matter known in the universe.

The brain is not sensitive to pain. Headache pain originates in the nerves, muscles, and tissues surrounding the skull, not from the brain.

The human brain is grayish-pink in color and has a texture much like tofu.

On average, a woman's brain makes up 2.5 percent of her body weight. A man's brain only contributes 2 percent of his body weight.

Men's brains are less well formed and shrink at a faster rate than women's.

The human brain continues to send out electrical wave signals for up to thirty-seven hours following death.

The human brain can record more than 86 million bits of information daily.

> The brain is more active sleeping than it is watching TV.

The left hemisphere of the brain controls language in 95 percent of right-handed people. In left-handed people, 70 percent have language controlled by the right hemisphere.

> Brain-wave activity in humans changes when they catch the punch line of a joke.

The short-term memory capacity for most people is between five and nine items or digits. This is one reason that phone numbers were kept to seven digits (not including area code).

> A sixty-year-old British woman is the first known case of a person born with phonagnosia, or the inability to identify and recognize voices, which was previously only known to occur in those who had suffered strokes or brain damage. The only speaking voice that the woman can recognize is the Scottish accent of actor Sean Connery.

EYES ON THE PRIZE

A bird's eye takes up about 50 percent of its head; the human eye takes up about 5 percent of the head. To be comparable to a bird's eyes, the eyes of a human being would have to be the size of baseballs.

Visual scientists have estimated that, by the age of sixty, human eyes have been exposed to more light energy than would be released by a nuclear blast.

The average adult eyeball weighs about one ounce.

The average duration of a single blink of the human eye is 0.3 seconds.

The average human eye can distinguish about five hundred different shades of gray.

The average human eyelash lives about 150 days.

There are 1,200,000 fibers in a human optic nerve.

The average person's field of vision encompasses a 200-degree-wide angle.

The iris of the human eye provides better identification than a fingerprint. A scan of the iris has 256 different unique characteristics. A fingerprint has only 40.

The human eyes can perceive more than 1 million simultaneous visual impressions and are able to discriminate among nearly 8 million gradations of color.

The average time between blinks of the eye is 2.8 seconds.

Uncontrollable winking is the physical symptom of those suffering from blepharospasms.

Given enough time to adjust, the human eye can, for a time, see almost as well as an owl's. Ultimately, as the amount of light decreases, an owl detects shapes after a human no longer can.

It takes the human eyes an hour to adapt completely to seeing in the dark. Once adapted, however, the eyes are about 100,000 times more sensitive to light than they are in bright sunlight.

While seven men in a hundred have some form of color blindness, only one woman in a thousand suffers from it. The most common form of color blindness is a red-green deficiency.

The lens of the eye steadily continues to grow throughout a person's life.

The human eye is continuously but imperceptibly moving. Muscle contractions cause it to quiver thirty to fifty times per second.

Ninety to 95 percent of all sensory perceptions are visual-based.

While reading, the eyes move in a series of jumps, called "fixations," from one clump of words to the next.

Some legally blind people can sense light, explaining their relative sync in biorhythms with sighted people.

The only part of the human body that has no blood supply is the cornea, which takes its oxygen directly from the air.

The retina of the eye—3.2 millimeters wide and 0.5 millimeters thick—can perceive and dissolve a new image every tenth of a second.

The medical term for a black eye is *bilateral periorbital hematoma*, while the medical term for cross-eye is *strabismus*.

Only about 6 percent of women fail to cry at least once a month, while 50 percent of men fail to cry that often.

Early students of forensics hoped that by photographing the eyes of murder victims they would see a reflection of the murderer lingering there.

WEIGHTY ISSUES

The average female between the ages of twenty and forty-four is more likely to be overweight than is a male in the same age category.

Some astrologists claim that people gain and lose weight in accordance with moon cycles.

The countries with the greatest obesity rates are in the South Pacific—Nauru (94.5 percent), followed by the Federated States of Micronesia (91.1 percent).

On average, adults spend seventy-seven minutes eating per day.

A person would have to play Ping-Pong for approximately twelve hours to burn enough calories to lose one pound.

The average adult has between 40 and 50 billion fat cells.

The higher the fat content in food, the longer it takes to digest.

The average woman consumes 2,000 calories a day, the average man about 2,500.

Staying warm in cold weather isn't easy. Up to 1,800 calories daily—90 percent of many people's energy intake—

may have to be burned to maintain a body temperature of 98.6°F.

Smaller animals tend to have lower metabolic rates because they have to work less to keep their bodies warm.

The hydrochloric acid of the human digestive process is so strong a corrosive that it easily can eat its way through the iron of a car body.

The human body needs twenty-four hours without exercise every week in order to cleanse itself of lactic acid and other waste products from exercise.

According to acupuncturists, the ear is an important area for controlling appetite.

The average digestive tract of an adult is thirty feet in length.

Couples who diet while on holiday argue three times more often than those who don't, and those who don't diet have three times as many romantic interludes.

GETTING AN EARFUL

The sound of a snore (up to eighty-nine decibels) can be almost as loud as the noise of a pneumatic drill (seventy to ninety decibels).

Normal hearing can detect sounds as soft as 10 decibels and as loud as 140 decibels.

When a person dies, hearing is generally the last sense to go. The first sense lost is usually sight, followed by taste, smell, and touch.

The human ear can distinguish more than fifteen different musical tones.

Loud talk can be ten times more distracting than the sound of a jackhammer.

HEART ATTACK

The average human heart beats about 100,000 times every day and 40 million times in a year. In approximately seventy years, the heart beats more than 2.5 billion times.

Two hundred and twenty beats per minute is the maximum heartbeat possible for a human.

In one hour, the heart produces enough energy to raise almost one ton of weight a yard off the ground.

It takes twenty-five to seventy-five watts of electricity to stop the human heart.

The human heart grows by development of cells, not cell multiplication.

Human heart valves are as thick as a piece of tissue paper.

The human heart is no bigger than a fist and yet is wrapped in so much muscle that it can continue pumping even if a third of its muscle mass is destroyed.

The heart beats faster during a brisk walk or a heated argument than during sex.

Sex, angry outbursts, and strenuous tennis are among the triggers identified as responsible for 17 percent of all heart attacks.

People who lose a friend, relative, or loved one face great physical risks and are more likely than normal to suffer a heart attack a day or two after the death.

BLOOD BANK

It takes from four to fifteen months for blood vessels to recuperate from simple sunburn.

Statistics show that pessimism raises blood pressure.

Cutting off the blood supply to the brain causes a loss of consciousness in ten seconds, with death occurring within minutes.

Human blood most closely resembles seawater in terms of chemical composition.

The average healthy person can lose as much as one-third of his or her blood without fatal results.

Men have more blood than women.

HAND-Y WORK

The slowest growing nail is the thumb's; the fastest growing nail is the middle finger's.

Nails grow one to two inches per year. It takes about three months to replace a fingernail.

Boys are more likely to be left-handed than girls.

ORGAN FARM

One individual organ transplant donor can provide organs, bone, and tissue for fifty or more people.

The human body can still survive even if the stomach, the spleen, most of the liver and intestines, one kidney, one lung, and every organ from the pelvic and groin area are removed.

If 80 percent of the liver were to be removed, the remaining part would continue to function. Within a few months, the liver would have reconstituted itself to its original size.

Women reject heart transplants more often than men.

THE SEA INSIDE

The loss of just 15 to 20 percent of the body's water can be fatal.

When the human body is dehydrated, its thirst mechanism shuts off, so if you are never thirsty, you need to drink more water.

Fingers and toes get wrinkled like prunes when soaked in water too long because the skin cells have absorbed some of the water.

LOST IN EMOTION

Recent studies conducted by scientists show that a sense of humor is dependent on nurture, not nature.

The period between the hours of four and six in the afternoon is when people are the most irritable.

The color light green is effective in relieving the feelings of homesickness.

Events such as pleasant family celebrations or evenings with friends boost the immune system for the following two days. Unpleasant moments have the opposite effect: negative events, such as being criticized at work, were found to weaken the immune function for one day afterward. However, some stress may be good for people. Rockefeller University scientists have determined that an acute episode of stress also boosts immunity, offering better protection against infection.

TAKE MY BREATH AWAY

In one minute of breathing, the average human takes in fourteen pints of air.

You can't kill yourself by holding your breath. At worst, you would lose consciousness and the lungs would start to breathe automatically.

An adult sitting in a relaxed position inhales approximately one pint of air with every breath.

Seeing another person yawn makes it likely that you will yawn yourself. Thinking about or even reading about yawning can set you off. People with mental disorders such as psychoses rarely yawn.

Because of their extreme elasticity, the lungs are one hundred times easier to blow up than a child's toy balloon.

The average person takes between twelve and eighteen breaths per minute.

Hiccups are caused by a sudden contraction of the diaphragm, which drags air into the lungs so fast that it snaps the vocal cords shut.

The rush of air produced by a cough moves at a speed approaching 600 miles per hour.

The fastest sneeze recorded traveled at 103.6 miles per hour.

SEX ED

Men can have 8 million genetically different sperm, and women a like number of egg types. Together they can produce 64 billion children with no genetic duplicates.

Puberty before the age of ten in a boy is called "precocious" puberty.

Men reach the peak of their sexual powers in their late teens or early twenties and then slowly begin to decline. Women, however, do not reach their sexual peak until their late twenties or early thirties and then remain at this level through their late fifties or early sixties.

Men who are exposed to a lot of toxic chemicals, high heat, and unusual pressures, such as those faced by jet pilots and deep-sea divers, are more prone to father girls than boys.

Men who take steroids to build muscle are believed to have extremely low sperm counts. After giving up steroids, it takes men one to three years to recover enough to father a child.

Eating garlic during pregnancy can cut the risk of raised blood pressure and protein retained in the urine, or preeclampsia.

The epididymis, the tube that carries spermatozoa, is fifteen to twenty feet long in an adult male.

There are fewer births nine months after a heat wave, with an increase of 53.6°F in summer temperatures reducing births the following spring by up to 6 percent. This could mean that high temperatures reduce people's sense of well-being, which could result in a reduction in sexual interest. On the other hand, lower sperm counts and higher rates of miscarriage have also been recorded during hot weather.

New York men have higher sperm counts and better semen quality than Los Angeles men. Medical experts believe the warm weather and higher pollution in Los Angeles might be the culprit behind the lower counts.

A parent's stress at the time of conception can play a major role in determining a baby's sex. The child tends to be the same sex as the parent who was under less stress.

A man's testicles produce 72 million sperm a day—enough in six weeks to impregnate the entire world's female population.

All the genetic material in the sperm and egg cells that produced the Earth's present population could fit into a space the size of an aspirin.

A baby girl is born with thousands of egg cells already in her ovaries.

A woman's arthritic pains will almost always disappear as soon as she becomes pregnant.

A majority of women unconsciously choose mates with a body odor that differs from their own natural scent, which ensures better immune protection for their children by giving the children a wider variety of genes.

Women who are vegetarians may be more likely to give birth to baby girls than boys.

Men are more fertile in the winter.

Pregnancy specialists warn that using fertility drugs give couples a one-in-four chance of a multiple birth.

Relative to its tiny size, the human sperm cell can swim 50 percent faster than an adult male can.

During pregnancy, the uterus expands to five hundred times its normal size.

MEDICAL ENCYCLOPEDIA

One in ten people suffers from some kind of phobia at some time in life.

Some psychologists contend that many people enjoy anxiety, based on the popularity of horror films and roller coasters.

The National Institute of Mental Health places fear of flying second only to fear of public speaking.

Fear of spiders (arachnophobia) is the most common phobia for people, followed by fear of snakes (ophidiophobia).

Mageirocophobia is the intense fear of having to cook.

If someone is androphobic, he or she has an extreme, irrational fear of men.

If you are afraid that you might die laughing, you are suffering from cherophobia.

Someone with an irrational fear of meat is carnophobic.

Gymnophobia is a fear of nakedness.

A person who is scoptophobic has an intense fear of being seen.

If a person is aerophobic, they have an irrational fear of drafts.

Dishabiliophobia is a fear of undressing in front of someone.

The characteristic red nose caused by broken capillaries, often caused by a person's excessive drinking over a prolonged period, is called rhinophyma, or "grog blossom."

"Buccula" is a little-used term for a person's double chin.

A nullipara is a woman who has never borne a child.

Zoanthropy is a form of mental disorder in which the patient imagines him- or herself to be a beast.

Tomatophagia is an unusual eating disorder—also known as pica—and is blamed on iron-deficiency anaemia. People with tomatophagia develop unusual cravings for such things as tomatoes, ice, detergent, starch, clay, or even dirt.

Zoonoses are animal diseases communicable to man.

Synesthesia is a rare condition in which the senses are combined. Synesthetes see words, taste colors and shapes, and feel flavors.

Someone who speaks through clenched teeth is called a dentiloquist.

THE NOSE KNOWS

One-quarter of the people who lose their sense of smell also lose their desire for sexual relations.

Some odor technicians in the perfume trade have the olfactory skill to distinguish nineteen thousand odors at various levels of intensity.

A human can detect one drop of perfume diffused throughout a three-room apartment.

By the age of twenty, most humans have lost up to 20 percent of their sense of smell. By the age of sixty, 60 percent is gone.

The nose cleans, warms, and humidifies more than five hundred cubic feet of air every day.

One in three male motorists picks his nose while driving.

About 25 percent of all adolescent and adult males never use deodorant.

DREAM A LITTLE DREAM

People dream an average of five times a night, and each subsequent dream is longer than the one preceding it.

There is no one who does not dream. Those who claim to have no dreams, laboratory tests have determined, simply forget their dreams more easily than others.

As much as 6 percent of the world's population may experience sleep paralysis—the inability to move and speak for several minutes after awakening.

On the average, a woman is three times more sensitive than a man to noises while sleeping.

Nineteen percent of people who snore are so loud that they can be heard through a closed door.

If the roof of your mouth is narrow, you are more prone to snoring, since you are not getting enough oxygen through your nose.

Women who snore regularly are at an increased risk of high blood pressure and cardiovascular disease.

While sleeping, one man in eight snores, and one in ten grinds his teeth.

A LIFETIME OF AVERAGES

The average person can live up to three days without any water intake.

The average able person will walk 115,000 miles in a lifetime, or around the world four and a half times.

The average life span of a fifteenth-century man in England was thirty years.

For more than a hundred thousand years, the maximum human life span has been 120 years.

The average person takes between eight thousand and ten thousand steps a day.

People who attend church, synagogue, or other religious services once a week live to an average age of eighty-two. Non-churchgoers live to an average age of seventy-five, or seven years less.

The average person receives eight birthday cards annually.

The average person spends thirty years being angry with a family member.

ANIMAL ATTRACTION

ALL CREATURES GREAT AND SMALL

Of all the life-forms that have ever existed on earth, 99 percent are now extinct.

The arctic fox often follows the polar bear, feeding on the abandoned carcasses of its kills.

The stomach of a giraffe has four chambers.

Baby squirrels are called kittens.

A raccoon appears to wash its food before eating it.

The jaguar is the largest of the American big cats and the third largest feline overall, after the tiger and the lion.

The elephant is the only mammal able to kneel on all fours.

Horses can sleep standing up.

The Falabella is the world's smallest breed of horse.

Coyotes mate for life.

A female walrus is called a cow.

A male guinea pig is called a boar.

Turkish van cats have a natural predilection for water.

A female mouse is called a doe.

The dingo is the only carnivore native to Australia.

In China the hedgehog is considered sacred and treated with respect.

The Chinese crested dog is hairless.

The wolverine is sometimes known as the glutton due to its enormous appetite.

In ancient Canadian legend, the turtle was the oldest and wisest creature on earth before man came to the Americas.

Turtles can breathe through their bottoms.

A unihemispheric slow wave sleep occurs when one half of an animal's brain sleeps while the other half stays alert. Birds, dolphins, and seals all exhibit this characteristic.

CHICK MAGNET

The chicken population of the world is more than double the human population.

Turkey skins are sometimes tanned and used to make cowboy boots and belts.

The pheasant originated in China.

The roadrunner is a member of the cuckoo family.

The nesting site of penguins is called a rookery.

DON'T HAVE A COW

Cows can smell odors six miles away.

The world's cattle population outnumbers the population of China.

It's possible to lead a cow upstairs but not downstairs.

Cows are milked for an average of three to four years.

The first cow in America arrived at the Jamestown colony in 1611.

The average body temperature of a cow is about 101.5°F.

There are approximately 350 "squirts" in a gallon of milk.

Wisconsin has the most dairy cows. Texas has the most beef cows.

GOING BATTY

Bats make up more than 23 percent of all known mammal species, with 980-plus species.

The largest bats have a wingspan of six feet. The "hog-nosed" bat's body is only one inch long, with a wingspan of three inches.

Some species of bats can live up to thirty-four years.

Some small animals like bats consume up to one and a half times their body weight in food every day. For the average male human, this would be equivalent to eating a thousand quarter-pound cheeseburgers daily.

FISHING FOR INFORMATION

Fish have no eyelids, as their eyes do not close.

Even the smallest catfish has 250,000 taste buds or more.

Seahorses are the only fish in which the head forms a right angle with the body.

Starfish don't have brains.

Spas in China offer fish pedicures, in which live fish eat away the dead skin on the feet.

Dolphins are the only species besides humans that have sex for pleasure.

INSECT-ASIDE

For every person on earth, there are 200 million insects.

The ant always falls over to its right side when intoxicated.

The part of a snail's body that remains inside the shell is called a mantle.

Researchers estimate that one of every three bites of food depends on the pollination of bees. This includes berries, fruits, nuts, almonds, and watermelons, among many others.

DOG DAYS

The Akita is the national dog of Japan. The care of these dogs is subsidized by the government if the owners become unable to care for them properly.

The Kangal Dog is the national dog of Turkey, but is not recognized as a breed by the English Kennel Club.

Dogs only have sweat glands between their paw pads.

A one-year-old dog is as physically mature as a fifteen-year-old human.

Dog nose prints are as unique as human fingerprints and can be used to identify them.

Dogs do not have an appendix.

HISTORICAL REFERENCE

FASHION FORWARD

The pharaohs of ancient Egypt wore garments made with thin threads of beaten gold, with some fabrics having up to five hundred gold threads per inch of cloth.

In ancient Egypt, priests plucked every hair from their bodies, eyebrows and eyelashes included.

In Britain, a green wedding dress was thought to be unlucky unless the bride was Irish. The expression that a woman had a "green gown" implied promiscuity, as the green staining of her clothing was the result of rolling about in grassy fields with a lover.

Courtesans in ancient Greece wore sandals with nails studded into the soles. Their footprints would leave the message "Follow me."

A merkin was a pubic wig originally worn by prostitutes.

More than one hundred years ago, the felt hatmakers of England used mercury to stabilize wool, with many eventually becoming poisoned by the fumes— as demonstrated by the Mad Hatter in Lewis Carroll's *Alice's Adventures in Wonderland*.

Iridescent beetle shells were the source of the earliest eye glitter ever used—devised by the ancient Egyptians.

As they consider giant noses a mark of great beauty, the San Blas Indian women of Panama paint black lines down the center of their noses to make them appear longer.

Thai women wear black only for funerals and periods of mourning.

In central Australia, it was once the custom for balding Aranda Aborigines to wear wigs made of emu feathers.

In India, men can wear pajamas in public as they are standard daytime apparel.

In Ethiopia, an old tradition requires the jewelry of a bride to be removed after her wedding. Its likeness is then tattooed on her skin.

A conventional sign of virginity in Tudor England was a high exposed bosom and a sleeve full to the wrists.

To prevent drowning, sailors once put a tattoo of a pig on one foot and a rooster on the other.

In one study, 3.9 percent of women said they don't wear underwear.

One out of ten people admit that they would buy an outfit intending to wear it once and return it.

MONEY TALKS

The first country to introduce paper money was China, in 812, but it wasn't until 1661 that another bank, in Sweden, issued banknotes.

In England in 1060, a coin was minted shaped like a clover. The user could break off any of the four leaves and use them as separate pieces of currency.

In Clarendon, Texas, lawyers must apparently accept eggs, chickens, or other produce, as well as money, as payment of legal fees.

Kettledrums were once used as currency on the island of Aler in Indonesia.

Until the nineteenth century, solid blocks of tea were used as money in Siberia.

The zloty ("golden") is the currency of Poland.

When invading Rome in 408 CE, the Goths demanded a ransom of three thousand peppercorns.

Twenty-five percent of women think money makes a man sexier.

A trillion dollars would be the equivalent of a stack of thousand-dollar bills 63 miles high, or a stack of twenty-dollar bills 3,150 miles high. Toward the end of George W. Bush's term as president, the national debt was the equivalent of a stack of twenty-dollar bills 30,240 miles high.

WE WISH YOU A MERRY CHRISTMAS

In 1752, eleven days were dropped from the year when the switch from the Julian calendar to the Gregorian calendar was made. The December 25 date was effectively moved back. Some Christian church sects, called old calendarists, still celebrate Christmas on January 7.

In the Black Forest area in Germany, religious families lay an extra place at the table for the Virgin Mary on Christmas Eve.

The traditional Armenian Christmas Eve meal consists of fried fish, lettuce, and spinach.

The ancient Norse associated mistletoe with their goddess of love, leading to the tradition of kissing under the mistletoe.

In Greek legend, malicious creatures called *kallikantzaroi* sometimes play troublesome pranks at Christmastime. One could burn either salt or an old shoe to get rid of them, as the stench would drive them off.

CHURCH CHATTER

The Lord's Prayer appears twice in the Bible—in Matthew 6 and Luke 11.

According to the Dead Sea Scrolls, the "Sermon on the Mount" passage of the Bible is an ancient Essene prayer dating hundreds of years before the birth of Christ.

Two books in the Bible, II Kings and Isaiah, contain very similar chapters.

The twenty-seven books of the Bible's New Testament are believed to have been written circa 50–100 CE, years after the death of Jesus.

Jesus gave St. Peter the name Cephas. It means "the rock."

The name Beelzebub means "lord of the flies."

In the Islamic religion, Israfil is the angel who will sound the trumpet announcing the end of the world.

The longest name in the Bible is Mahershalalbaz.

A survey once disclosed that 12 percent of Americans believe that Joan of Arc was Noah's wife.

New Zealand has ordained women priests since the 1968.

More than 95 percent of the population of Greece belongs to the Greek Orthodox Church.

The Roman Catholic population of the world is larger than that of all other Christian sects combined.

Nuns have an average life expectancy of seventy-seven years, the longest of any group in the United States.

THE SAINTS GO MARCHING

Roman Emperor Nero sentenced St. Peter to crucifixion.

St. Jude is the patron saint of hopeless causes.

There are many patron saints for human physical afflictions, including St. James the Greater, patron saint of rheumatoid sufferers; St. Teresa of Avila, the patron saints of headaches; St. Apollonia, patron saint of tooth-aches; and St. Genevieve, patron saint of fevers.

St. Columba and his followers first claimed to see the Loch Ness Monster in 565 CE.

St. George, the patron saint of England, never actually visited England.

St. John was the only one of the Twelve Apostles to die a natural death.

OMEN OVERLOAD

In Scotland, it is believed that if someone walks any distance between two redheaded girls, it is a sign that he or she will soon be wealthy.

In Russia, when someone is leaving for a trip, this person and a close friend or spouse sits in silence on the traveler's packed suitcases before he or she departs. It is believed that this moment of togetherness will cause the traveler to have a safe journey.

In Greece, overturned shoes are considered omens of death or very bad luck. If you take them off and this happens accidentally, turn them over immediately, say *skorda* ("garlic"), and spit once or twice.

A hot cross bun kept from one Good Friday to the next was once considered a lucky charm in England;

it was not supposed to grow moldy and was used as a charm against shipwreck. Good Friday bread, when hung over the chimneypiece, was supposed to guarantee that all bread baked after that would be perfect.

In Japan, frogs are symbols of good luck. The dragonfly symbolizes good luck, courage, and manliness. Japanese warriors customarily wore the dragonfly emblem in battle.

A dinner party consisting of thirteen people during the Middle Ages was the worst of omens, as it foretold of the impending death of one in the group.

In Britain, witches were once said to disguise themselves as cats, so many people refused to talk near a cat for fear that a witch would learn their secrets.

According to old farmers' traditions, the best time of the day to select a new pair of shoes is in the afternoon, when the exercise of the day has stretched the muscles to their largest extent.

In Britain, a horseshoe was thought to be a guardian against all evil forces. Inhabitants of the spirit world were supposed to flee from the sight of cold iron.

In America, when moving to a new home, the cat should be put in through the window, not the door.

Saying "rabbit, rabbit" upon waking on the first day of every month is supposed to bring good luck for that month. To counteract forgetting to say it, one can say it backward, or say "moose, moose" on the second day of the month.

LAST RITES

It is estimated that 74 billion human beings have been born and died in the last 500,000 years.

University graduates live longer than people who did not complete school.

The ancient Egyptians placed obsidian balls, or occasionally brass balls, in the eye sockets of mummies.

Jerusalem's Church of the Holy Sepulchre marks the spot where Joseph of Arimathea buried Jesus.

In Orthodox Judaism, the law of Halakha forbids the practice of cremation.

When Richard II died, in 1400, a hole was left in the side of his tomb so that people could touch his royal head. However, 376 years later, it is said that a schoolboy took advantage of this and stole his jaw-bone.

Humphrey Bogart's ashes are in an urn that also contains a small gold whistle. Lauren Bacall had the whistle inscribed, "If you need anything, just whistle"—the words she spoke to him in their first film together, *To Have and Have Not*.

Comedian George Carlin once said he wanted his tombstone to read, "Geez, he was just here a minute ago."

Dorothy Parker wanted "This is on me" on her tombstone.

In 1973, Swedish confectionery salesman Roland Ohisson was buried in a coffin made entirely of chocolate.

After the death of Alexander the Great, his remains were preserved in a huge crock of honey.

Dr. Fredric J. Bauer, the inventor of the Pringles potato chip tube, requested that his family bury his remains inside his proudest invention.

Until the 1950s, Tibetans disposed of their dead by taking the body up a hill, hacking it into little pieces, and feeding the remains to the birds.

When a man of the Danakil tribesmen of Ethiopia dies, his grave is marked with a stone for every man he has killed.

The Japanese cremate 93 percent of their dead, compared with Great Britain, at 67 percent, and the United States, at just over 12 percent.

In America and England, witches were hanged, not burned.

In Mexico and Chile, yellow flowers are a sign of grieving or separation.

The Los Angeles County Department of Coroner is the second largest coroner's department in the nation and handles nineteen thousand cases a year, 10 percent of them homicides. It is the only one in the world with a gift shop, aptly named Skeletons in the Closet.

LIFE AFTER DEATH

Lawrence of Arabia's ghost is said to be heard riding his motorcycle near his house in Dorset, England, where he died in a motorcycle accident.

Actor Montgomery Clift is said to haunt room number 928 of the Roosevelt Hotel in Hollywood, which was home to him for three months while filming

From Here to Eternity. Hotel guests and employees have reported sensing the actor's presence, or have heard him reciting his lines.

The Roosevelt Hotel is also said to be haunted by the ghost of Marilyn Monroe.

Windsor Castle is home to the ghosts of King Henry VIII, Queen Elizabeth I, King Charles I, and King George III. King Henry is supposed to haunt the cloisters near the deanery with ghostly groans and the sound of dragging footsteps.

A CUT ABOVE

A scientist condemned to death by guillotine in the 1700s supposedly told his assistant to watch his head after he was decapitated, as he would blink as many times as he could to prove that the head remains conscious about fifteen to twenty seconds after decapitation. The assistant reported counting fifteen to twenty blinks.

The head of executed murderer Charlotte Corday supposedly blushed and looked indignant when the executioner slapped the cheek after decapitation.

After two rivals were guillotined during the French Revolution and their heads were placed in one sack, one head supposedly bit the other so hard they couldn't be separated.

In 1905 a doctor claimed that when he called the name of an executed murderer just after decapitation, the head opened its eyes and focused on him.

A soldier who was in a car accident in Korea with a friend noted that the friend's head attempted to speak and look around for several seconds after decapitation.

Monarch Musings

ROYAL RESIDENCES

George II died in his water closet at Kensington Palace, deterring later monarchs from living there.

Queen Victoria referred to Kensington Palace as "the poor old palace."

Greenwich Palace was Henry VIII's favorite residence.

Extensions to Greenwich Palace conflicted with the main road from Deptford to Woolwich, so it was built on either side, with a bridge joining the two halves until the road was diverted.

The drains at Windsor Castle were faulty, allegedly causing the death of Prince Albert.

It was quite common for Westminster Palace to flood

with mud and fish from the River Thames, and once rowing boats had to be used in the Great Hall.

William III and his wife Mary hated Whitehall Palace, as it was bad for William's asthma.

Whitehall Palace once contained a chemical laboratory.

William IV considered turning Buckingham Palace into army barracks.

The Tower of London was once used as a zoo.

The first prisoner in the Tower of London, Ranulf Flambard, bishop of Durham, escaped down a rope smuggled to him in a wine casket.

Queen Anne banned the wearing of spectacles, inappropriate wigs, and the smoking of pipes from St. James's Palace.

Hot water and clean linens were sent to Prince Albert's room every morning after his death. The glass he sipped his last medicine from lay unmoved on the table next to his bed for forty years.

EXERTING AUTHORITY

Henry VIII was probably the most athletic monarch, enjoying tennis, archery, hunting, and wrestling.

Charles II was a keen tennis player and would weigh himself before and after every game to see how much weight he had lost.

KINGS' BEST FRIENDS

Charles II had many dogs, and at official meetings of state he preferred playing with them to listening to the discussion.

Henry III kept a quartet of lions in the Tower of London. They were allegedly called Fanny, Miss Fanny, Miss Howe, and Miss Fanny Howe.

Charles I's dog accompanied him to his execution.

Henry III received a polar bear from the king of Norway. It was allowed to hunt for fish in the River Thames, on the end of a long rope.

The first elephant in England was a gift to King Henry III from the King Louis IX of France.

PROPER BEHAVIOR

James I introduced a swear box to St. James's Palace, and all the money deposited into it by transgressing parishioners was given to the poor.

George II sold tickets to allow the public to watch the king and queen eat.

At royal banquets, the salt cellar was always the first thing to be laid on the table.

James VI banned the use of the surname Mac-Gregor.

The only house in England that the queen may not enter is the House of Commons, as she is not a commoner.

Prince Charles and Prince William never travel on the same plane as a precaution against a potential crash.

THE FAMILY JEWELS

The Duchess of Windsor's single-strand natural-pearl-and-diamond necklace was auctioned at Sotheby's in 1987 and purchased by designer Calvin Klein for his wife, Kelly.

The Sovereign's Scepter contains the 530-carat Star of Africa diamond, also known as Cullinan I.

There are 2,868 diamonds, 273 pearls, 17 sapphires, 11 emeralds, and 5 rubies on Britain's Imperial State Crown. This includes the Lesser Star of Africa.

THE WORLD WE KNOW

PERSONS OF INTEREST

Adolf Hitler was fascinated by hands. He kept a book of pictures and drawings of hands belonging to famous people throughout history. He was convinced that his own hands bore a great resemblance to those of Frederick the Great, one of his heroes.

Adolf Hitler's third-grade school report remarked that he was "bad tempered" and fancied himself as a leader.

As Hitler's body was never found, a German court officially declared Hitler dead in 1956.

Howard Hughes became so compulsive about germs that he used to spend hours swabbing his arms over and over again with rubbing alcohol. Although he had fifteen personal attendants and three doctors on full-time duty, he died of neglect and malnutrition, caused by his intense desire to be left alone.

Howard Hughes never once attended a board of directors meeting, or any sort of meeting, at any of the companies he owned.

In 1994, Chicago artist Dwight Kalb sent talk show host David Letterman a statue of Madonna made of 180 pounds of ham.

The most ill-fated wives of Henry VIII of England, the decapitated Catherine Howard and Anne Boleyn, were first cousins. Catherine's father, Lord Edmund Howard, was the brother of Anne Boleyn's mother, Lady Elizabeth Howard.

King Louis XIV of France established in his court the position of royal chocolate maker to the king.

When Napoleon wore black silk handkerchiefs around his neck during a battle, he always won. At Waterloo, he wore a white cravat and lost the battle.

Napoleon reportedly carried chocolate on all his military campaigns.

On average, Elizabeth Taylor has remarried every four years, five months.

Pontius Pilate was born in Scotland.

Justin Timberlake's half-eaten french toast sold for more than $3,000 on eBay.

The makeup entrepreneur Elizabeth Arden's real name was Florence Nightingale Graham, but she changed it after a business partnership dissolved in the early 1900s.

Charles Darwin cured his snuff habit by keeping his snuffbox in the basement and the key for the snuff-box in the attic.

Voltaire drank between fifty and seventy-two cups of coffee every day.

Manfredo Settala is the only person in all recorded history that has been killed by a meteorite, in 1680.

Leonardo da Vinci was the first person to suggest using contact lenses for vision, in 1508.

Leonardo da Vinci wrote notebook entries in backward script, a trick that kept many of his observations from being widely known until decades after his death. It is believed that he was hiding his scientific ideas from the powerful Roman Catholic Church, whose teachings sometimes disagreed with what da Vinci observed.

Rembrandt, the Dutch painter, died almost penniless at the age of sixty-three.

Comedy team Abbott and Costello had an insurance policy to cover themselves financially in the event they had an argument with each other.

The Nestlé family hasn't run Nestlé since 1875.

Heavyweight boxing champion George Foreman has five sons, named George, George Jr., George III, George IV, George V, and George VI.

Queen Elizabeth I named a man as the official uncorker of bottles, and passed a law that stated all bottles found washed up on beaches had to be opened by him and no one else, in case they contained sensitive military messages. The penalty for anyone else opening a bottle was the death sentence.

Karl Marx rarely took a bath and suffered from boils most of his life.

Empress Matilda of England supposedly escaped Oxford in 1142 by journeying across the snow-covered countryside in a white cape. A year earlier she had escaped another siege by disguising herself as a corpse and being carried out for burial.

Robert Peary, discoverer of the North Pole, included a photograph of his nude mistress in a book about his travels.

King John did not sign the Magna Carta in 1215, as he could not write his name. Instead he placed his seal on it.

Notorious bootlegger Al Capone made $50 million during Prohibition.

Peter the Great hated the Kremlin, where, as a child, he had witnessed the brutal torture and murder of his mother's family.

King George I could not speak English, as he was born and raised in Germany, so he left the running of the country to his ministers.

A drinking cup used by Napoleon was made from the skull of the famous Italian adventurer Cagliostro.

Pamela Anderson is Canada's Centennial Baby, being the first baby born on the centennial anniversary of Canada's independence.

French chemist Louis Pasteur had an obsessive fear of dirt and infection. He would never shake hands, would carefully wipe his plate and glass before dining, and would sneak a microscope under his coat into friends' houses and then examine the food they served to make sure it was safe from germs.

Andrew Carnegie, one of the richest Americans ever, never carried any cash. He was once sent off a London train because he did not have the fare.

While he was a member of Parliament, Sir Isaac Newton's only recorded utterance was a request to open the window.

Cleopatra tested the efficacy of her poisons by giving them to slaves.

American showman P. T. Barnum had his obituary published before his death.

Henry Ford was obsessed with soybeans. He ordered many Ford auto parts to be made from soy-derived plastic and once wore a suit and tie made from soy-based material.

Albert Einstein reportedly had a huge crush on film star Marilyn Monroe.

Albert Einstein was reluctant to sign autographs, and charged people a dollar before signing anything. He gave the dollars to charity.

The younger of Albert Einstein's two sons was a schizo-phrenic.

Lady Diana Spencer was the first Englishwoman commoner in three hundred years to marry an heir to the British throne.

As a boy, Charles Darwin was so enamored with chemistry that his young friends nicknamed him "Gas."

Napoleon suffered from ailurophobia, the fear of cats.

Catherine II of Russia kept her wigmaker in an iron cage in her bedroom for more than three years.

Emerson Moser, Crayola's senior crayon maker, revealed upon his retirement that he was blue-green color-blind and couldn't see all the colors.

Xerxes, king of Persia, became so angry at the sea when it destroyed his fleet during a storm that he had his army beat it with sticks.

Martha Jane Burke, better known as Calamity Jane, was married twelve times.

Telephone inventor Alexander Graham Bell had an odd habit of drinking his soup through a glass straw.

Jesse James would run back home to his mother

following a crime. His obsessive love for his mother extended to him marrying a woman named Zerelda, the same name as his mother's and one that was uncommon in the 1800s.

When he was a boy, Thomas Edison suffered a permanent hearing loss following scarlet fever and various untreated ear infections.

The Roman emperor Nero married his male slave Scorus in a public ceremony.

The pioneering scientist Marie Curie was not allowed to become a member of the prestigious French Academy because she was a woman.

During the seventeenth century, the sultan of Turkey ordered that his entire harem of women be drowned and replaced with a new one.

Henry VII was the only British king to be crowned on the field of battle.

Julius Caesar wore a laurel wreath to cover the onset of baldness.

As of 2008 there were six reigning queens in Europe: Queen Elizabeth II of the United Kingdom; Queen Sofia of Spain; Queen Beatrix of the Netherlands; Queen

Margrethe II of Denmark; Queen Silvia of Sweden; and Queen Fabiola of Belgium.

Julius Caesar, Martin Luther, Emily Dickinson, and Marilyn Monroe all suffered from Ménière's disease. It is a disorder of the hearing and balance senses, causing progressive deafness and attacks of tinnitus and vertigo.

To help create her signature sexy walk, Marilyn Monroe sawed off part of the heel of one shoe.

Socrates taught Plato, who in turn taught Aristotle.

Linus Pauling is the only man ever to win two individual Nobel prizes; one for peace, the other for chemistry.

Christian Barnard of South Africa performed the first heart transplant in 1967. The operation lasted nine hours and required a team of thirty people.

Nathuran Godse assassinated Gandhi in 1948.

Malcolm X's daughter Qubilah Bahiyah Shabazz was charged with allegedly hiring a hitman to kill the leader of the Nation of Islam.

When Neil Armstrong and Buzz Aldrin walked on the moon in 1969, Michael Collins was left behind in the command module.

Stella Rimington was the first woman to head the British Secret Service MI5.

TV chef and cookbook author Julia Child was revealed in 2008 to be part of a World War II-era U.S. spy ring.

🌰 ROOMS TO SPARE

The burglars who broke into the office building in the Watergate Hotel complex during the Nixon administration actually slept in rooms 214 and 314 of the hotel.

Anna Nicole Smith took her fatal overdose in room 607 of the Seminole Hard Rock Hotel in Florida.

Bungalow 3 at the Chateau Marmont in Los Angeles is available for $1,700 a night for any guest who wants to sleep in the room where actor John Belushi died of a drug overdose.

Room 871 at the Mayflower Hotel in Washington, DC, was the regular meeting place for guest George Fox—also known as Client 9, or former New York governor Eliot Spitzer—and his secret call girl.

Sid Vicious of the Sex Pistols was accused of stabbing his girlfriend Nancy Spungen in room 100 of the Hotel Chelsea.

All the rooms at the Lodge & Spa at Cordillera in Colorado were renumbered after basketball player Kobe Bryant was accused of raping a woman in room 35.

Another hotel, the Sheraton Sand Key Resort in Florida, kept room 538 available so guests could stay in the same room where televangelist Jim Bakker was accused of raping a church secretary.

POPULATION DENSITY

The population of the entire world in 5000 BCE was about 5 million. Now it is approximately 6.5 billion.

The world's population grows by 100 million each year.

There are 106 boys born for every 100 girls.

Half of the world's population lives in cities and towns.

Half the world's population is under twenty-five years of age.

Roughly 40 percent of the unemployed population of the world is under fifteen years of age.

Nearly half the population of Alaska lives in one city, Anchorage.

About 70 percent of Australia's Aboriginals live in towns and cities.

Eighty percent of the Australian population lives in the cities along the coast.

One in five people in the world's population lives in China.

Sheep outnumber people four to one in Wales.

The population of Colombia doubles every twenty-two years.

The area of Greater Tokyo—meaning the city, its port, Yokohama, and the suburban prefectures of Saitama, Chiba, and Kanagawa—contains less than 4 percent of Japan's land area, but fully one-quarter of its 123-plus million people.

Britain is roughly nine times more densely populated than America, with 588 people per square mile as compared with America's 65 people per square mile.

THE LIVES WE LEAD

More than 50 percent of the people in the world have never made or received a telephone call.

Smokers eat more sugar than nonsmokers do.

The people killed most often during bank robberies are the robbers.

Someone's gender can be guessed with 95 percent accuracy just by smelling his or her breath.

Ten percent of *Star Trek* fans replace the lenses on their glasses every five years, whether they need to or not.

People who are lying tend to look up and to the left.

Boys who have unusual first names are more likely to have mental problems than boys with conventional names.

One in three consumers pays off his or her credit card bill every month.

One in three snakebite victims is drunk. One in five is tattooed.

More than 50 percent of lottery players go back to work after winning the jackpot.

Children who are breast-fed tend to score higher on IQ tests than children who are not.

Male hospital patients tend to fall out of bed twice as often as female hospital patients.

We shed about 700,000 of our own skin flakes each day.

Astronauts get taller when they are in space.

When people are wide awake, alert, and mentally active, they are still only 25 percent aware of what various parts of their bodies are doing.

It's been estimated that men have been riding horses for more than three thousand years.

People who have computers in their homes tend to watch 40 percent less television than average.

People overwhelmingly tend to marry partners who live near them.

Young children are poisoned by houseplants more often than by detergents and other chemicals.

Men more often dream about their male heroes, bosses, friends, or role models than about women.

Each morning more than a third of all adults hit their alarm clock's "snooze" button an average of three times before they get up. Those people most guilty of snatching some extra sleep are in the twenty-five to thirty-four age bracket, at 57 percent.

Teenagers often have episodes of anger and negativity in which they slam doors and scream tirades, lasting an average of fifteen minutes.

Adults spend an average of sixteen times as many hours

selecting clothes (145.6 hours a year) as they do on planning their retirement.

The most popular form of hair removal among women is shaving, with 70 percent of women choosing this method.

Only 29 percent of married couples agree on most political issues.

Thirty-nine percent of people admit that, as guests, they have snooped in their host's medicine cabinets.

More than 50 percent of adults say that children should not be paid money for getting good grades in school.

Six percent of people that file for bankruptcy do so because they cannot stand bill collectors.

NEWSWORTHY

A German soldier was riding in the backseat of a World War I plane when the engine suddenly stalled and he fell out of his seat while more than two miles aboveground. As he was falling, the plane started falling too, and he was blown back into his own seat by the wind.

In 1949, Jack Wurm, an unemployed man, was aimlessly walking on a California beach when he came across a washed-up bottle containing this message: "To avoid confusion, I leave my entire estate to the lucky person who finds this bottle and to my attorney, Barry Cohen, share and share alike. Daisy Alexander, June 20, 1937." It was not a hoax and Mr. Wurm received more than $6 million from the Alexander estate.

A Japanese priest set a kimono on fire in Tokyo in 1657 because it carried bad luck. The flames spread until over 10,000 buildings were destroyed and 100,000 people died.

The most children born from the same mother, at one time, were decaplets. Born in Brazil, in 1946, eight girls and two boys were delivered.

In 2008 a Japanese man found an unemployed, homeless woman living in an unused closet in his house. Police suspected she had been living there undetected for months before the man figured out why food kept disappearing from his kitchen while he was at work.

Two animal rights protesters were protesting at the cruelty of sending pigs to a slaughterhouse in Bonn. Suddenly the pigs—all two thousand of them— escaped through a broken fence and stampeded, trampling the two helpless protesters to death.

One lady had her husband's ashes made into an egg

timer so that, even in death, he could still "help" in the kitchen.

Iraqi terrorist Khay Rahnajet didn't pay enough postage on a letter bomb. It came back with "return to sender" stamped on it. Forgetting it was the bomb, he opened it and was blown to bits.

When a thief was surprised while robbing a house in Antwerp, Belgium, he fled out of the back door, clambered over a nine-foot wall, dropped down, and found himself in the city prison.

A psychology student in New York once rented out her spare room to a carpenter in order to nag him constantly and study his reactions. After weeks of needling, he snapped and beat her repeatedly with an axe, leaving her brain-damaged.

On his way home to visit his parents, a Harvard student fell between two railroad cars at the station in Jersey City, New Jersey, and was rescued by an actor. The student was Robert Lincoln, heading for 1600 Pennsylvania Avenue. The actor was Edwin Booth, the brother of the man who, a few weeks later, would murder Robert's father, Abraham Lincoln.

In 1983, a woman was laid out in her coffin, presumed dead of heart disease. As mourners watched, she suddenly sat up. Her daughter dropped dead of fright.

A man hit by a car in New York in 1977 got up uninjured, but lay back down in front of the car when a bystander told him to pretend he was hurt so he could collect insurance money. The car rolled forward and crushed him to death.

A British couple was forced in 2008 to paint their medieval home "Suffolk pink" in order to add to the village's historical accuracy.

A woman in Utah once stole two fourteen-carat gold bracelets from a pawnshop by swallowing them. The bracelets, valued around $2,000, were eventually recovered . . . somehow.

A Cambodian couple who decided to separate literally divided their home because going to court to split their possessions would be too expensive. The wife kept the half that was left standing and the husband transferred his half to a nearby field.

German pop star Ramma Damma legally married a pineapple in Gretna Green, Scotland, in 1970. He purchased the pineapple for about $16 because he wanted to make sure his bride wasn't cheap.

During the 2008 presidential election, a family erected an Internet webcam to keep their Barack Obama yard sign from getting stolen. By the end of the election, more than forty thousand people across the world were taking shifts watching online to guard the sign.

POLITICAL PRISONERS

When Andrew Jackson ran for president against John Quincy Adams in 1828, his campaign slogan was "Adams can write, but Jackson can fight!" (Jackson won, though Adams had beaten him four years earlier.)

Thomas Jefferson once called John Adams a "howling hermaphrodite." Jefferson's own opponents charged that if he won the presidency, rape and incest would be taught in schools.

Robert Todd Lincoln, son of Abraham Lincoln, was present at the assassinations of three presidents: his father's, President Garfield's, and President McKinley's. After the last shooting, he refused ever to attend a state affair again.

President Lincoln's advisor during the Civil War, Frederick Douglass, was born a slave.

James Garfield was the first president known to have been caught cheating on his wife, with an 18-year-old New Yorker.

Grover Cleveland had an illegitimate child with a store clerk. When he became president, the child went to an orphanage, and the mother went to an insane asylum.

John F. Kennedy was the first Catholic president of the United States.

Ronald Reagan was a sports commentator before becoming a Hollywood actor.

A young Ronald Reagan once advertised Chesterfield cigarettes.

Ronald Reagan's Scottish terriers were called Scotch and Soda.

Rumor has it that when Republican president George W. Bush's staff moved into the White House, they found that departing Democratic president Bill Clinton's staff had removed the letter W from some computer keyboards.

During the 2008 presidential election a man named his newborn daughter Sarah McCain Palin after the Republican nominees without his wife's knowledge. She wanted to name the child Ava Grace.

NO, HE CAN'T

Barack Obama once applied to appear in a pinup calendar at Harvard but was rejected by the all-female committee.

MIND YOUR MANNERS

In China, it is unwise to give the gift of a clock, as to the older Chinese generation a clock is a symbol of bad luck.

In Pakistan, it is rude to show the soles of your feet or point a foot when you are sitting on the floor.

It is considered polite in Japan to initially refuse someone's offer of help. An offer is normally made three times.

In Zambia, hand shaking with the left hand supporting the right is common, while direct eye contact should not be made with members of the opposite sex.

In South America, it would be rude not to ask a man about his wife and children. In most Arab countries, it would be rude to do so.

The "fingers circle" gesture is the British sign for "OK," but in Brazil and Germany, the gesture is considered vulgar or obscene. The gesture is also considered impolite in Greece and Russia, while in Japan it means "money." In Southern France, the "fingers circle" sign signifies "worthless" or "zero."

In Tibet, it's good manners to stick out your tongue at your guests.

In Western culture, spitting is rude, but it is common as a Russian gesture to ward off bad luck or to express the hope for continued good fortune. A Russian individual will spit three times over his or her left shoulder.

In Thailand, the left hand is considered unclean, so should not be used when eating. Also, pointing with one finger is considered rude and is only done when pointing to objects or animals, never humans.

When members of the Western African Wodaabe tribe greet each other, they may not look each other directly in the eyes. Also, during daylight hours, a man cannot call his wife by her name, hold her hand in public, or speak to her in a personal way.

In Sweden, when you are leaving someone's home, you must not put your coat on until you are at the doorway, as to do so earlier suggests an eagerness to leave.

In Germany, shaking hands with the other hand in a pocket is considered impolite.

In France and Belgium, snapping the fingers of both hands has a vulgar meaning.

In Mali, a man will only shake hands with a woman if she offers her hand first. The handshake is often done with the left hand touching the other person's elbow as well.

TABLE TALK

In Jordan, when a host asks a visitor to stay for dinner it is customary to refuse twice before accepting. Unless the host insists numerous times, seconds of any dish offered should also be refused, and even then accepted only with a slight air of reluctance.

In Poland, hospitality calls for plenty of food being offered. The guest who declines is rude and the guest who grabs food without being encouraged disgraces himself.

Some restaurants in Kyoto, Japan, have a custom called *ichigensan okotowari*, which means that you must be introduced by someone to be welcomed. As a result, the restaurant is able to give its warmest hospitality and services to all its customers. Business cards are preferred to credit cards—most establishments will only accept cash.

Before eating, Japanese people say *itadakimasu*, meaning "I receive this food," an expression of thanks to whomever worked to prepare the meal.

The Japanese have many rules for the correct use of

chopsticks. Improper use includes wandering the chopsticks over several foods without decision (*mayoibashi*) and licking the ends of chopsticks (*neburibashi*), which is considered unforgivable. Similarly, chopsticks must never be used to point at somebody or be left standing up out of the food.

In ancient Rome, wealthy Romans always drank from goblets made of quartz crystal, as they believed the transparent mineral was a safeguard against their enemies. Legend had it that a cup carved from quartz would not hold poison.

In Egypt, it is customary to take a gift of flowers or chocolates when invited to dinner. The giving and receiving of gifts should be done with both hands or with the right hand—never with the left.

In Iceland, tipping at a restaurant is considered an insult.

The fork was not common in Western Europe until the tenth century, and fork-and-knife pairs were not in general use.

The ancient Egyptians trained baboons to wait on tables.

COUPLING UP

A prerequisite for a first date in Russia is buying carnations or roses, which must be given in odd numbers. Flowers given in even numbers are reserved for funerals.

A couple living together for two years in Russia is considered married. This is called a citizen marriage.

Ancient Greeks considered the philtrum, the indentation in the middle area between the nose and the upper lip, to be one of the body's most erogenous zones.

In Greece, the names of all single female friends and relatives of the bride are written on the sole of her shoe. Those whose names have worn off by the end of the wedding are said to be the next in line for marriage.

A wedding custom in early Yorkshire involved a plate holding wedding cake being thrown out of the window as the bride returned to her parental home after the wedding. If the plate broke, she would enjoy a happy future with her husband; if the plate remained intact, her future was bleak.

It was once the custom for French brides to step on an egg before crossing the threshold of their new homes.

In Anglo-Saxon times, brides were often kidnapped

before a wedding, and brawls during the service were common. For this reason a bride stood to the groom's left at a wedding so that his sword hand would be free. This also explains why the best man stands with the groom: the tribe's best warrior was there to help the groom defend the bride.

Finns count the number of grains of rice in the bride's hair to predict the number of children a newlywed couple will have. Czechs send off the newlyweds under a barrage of peas, while Italians throw sugared almonds.

Finding alternatives to rice showers at weddings is a tricky business. In 2008 two Texas women were badly injured while trying to light celebratory sparklers to send off the bride and groom. At a Russian wedding in Chechnya a guest threw an armed hand grenade into the unsuspecting crowd, injuring a dozen people.

According to old farmers' traditions, to test your love, you and your lover should each place an acorn in water. If they swim together, your love is true; if they drift apart, so will you.

In ancient Sparta, married men were not allowed to live with their wives until they turned thirty.

The women of the Tiwi tribe in the South Pacific are married at birth.

In India, people are legally allowed to marry a dog.

More than 20 percent of men and 10 percent of women say they've forgotten their wedding anniversary at least once.

It was Queen Victoria who made white wedding dresses fashionable. Before she wore a white dress for her 1840 wedding to Prince Albert, brides wore whatever was the nicest dress in their closet, in any color, including black. They also piled on as many furs and velvet as possible to display their family's wealth.

One explanation for the popularity of the wedding veil is its past utilization as a way to hide an unattractive bride from her new husband until the marriage "transaction" was complete.

Bridesmaid dresses and groomsman tuxes were originally supposed to be similar to the bride and groom's clothing in order to trick the eyes of evil spirits and jealous ex-lovers.

The maid of honor used to be responsible for making and hanging all of the wedding decorations herself.

To ward off evil spirits, a bride used to carry bunches of herbs, which eventually were replaced by flower bouquets.

A bride should be carried over the threshold so that evil spirits won't trip her and cause her bad luck.

LANDMASSES

All the Earth's continents, except Antarctica, are wider at the north than in the south.

Antarctica is the only land on the planet that is not owned by any country.

The tallest sand dunes in the world are in the Sahara Desert and the Badain Jaran Desert of China. The dunes have enough sand in them to bury the Great Pyramids of Egypt and the Eiffel Tower.

Airborne sand from the Sahara Desert has been picked up two thousand miles over the ocean.

Canada and the United States have the longest shared border of any two nations in the world.

China has the most borders with other countries.

Approximately one-third of Greenland, the world's largest island, is national park.

Greenland has more ice on it than Iceland does, while Iceland has more grass and trees than Greenland.

Venice consists of 118 islands linked by four hundred bridges.

Nicaragua is the largest and most sparsely populated state in Central America.

The bulk of the island of Tenerife is the volcanic mountain Mount Eide.

Panama is the only place in the world where someone can see the sun rise over the Pacific Ocean and set over the Atlantic.

🌰 ALSO KNOWN AS . . .

Himalayas means "abode of snow."

Shanghai is sometimes called the "Paris of the East" and the "Whore of China."

France is sometimes called the "Hexagon" because it is roughly six-sided.

Zaire was formerly known as the Belgian Congo.

The Canary Islands were once known as Blessed or Fortunate Isles.

The country of Tanzania has an island called Mafia.

Stockholm is known as the "Venice of the North."

The Romany people were wrongly thought to have come from Egypt, earning them the nickname "Gypsies."

There are castles on the River Rhine in Germany called the Cat and Mouse Castles.

The full name for Britain, the United Kingdom of Great Britain and Northern Ireland, is the third longest country name in the world.

The Spanish Steps are actually in Rome.

In 1939, a group of business and political leaders in Sheridan, Wyoming, planned to break off huge chunks of Wyoming, South Dakota, and Montana and form a new state, to be called Absaroka. They got as far as distributing license plates and crowning a Miss Absaroka 1939. There was even an Absarokan state visit, when the king of Norway made a swing through Montana.

WET WORLDS

All the landmass of the Earth and then some could fit into the Pacific Ocean.

At about 200 million years of age, the Atlantic Ocean is the youngest of the world's oceans.

The Republic of Kiribati, an island nation in the Pacific Ocean, is expected to be the first country in which land territory disappears due to global climate change, with the entire nation submerged within a century. The government has asked neighboring Australia and New Zealand to accept Kiribati citizens as permanent refugees.

There are no rivers or permanent bodies of water in Saudi Arabia.

The Amazon River's flow is twelve times that of the Mississippi.

BUILDING CODES

The Plaza Hotel, which has been owned by families such as the Hiltons and the Trumps, was sold by Donald Trump to a Saudi prince and a Singapore hotel chain. Now it's owned by an Israeli billionaire.

The Flatiron Building was used as the *Daily Bugle* building in the *Spider-Man* films. It is primarily owned by an Italian real estate investor.

The Chrysler Building, briefly the world's tallest building, has gargoyles designed for its original tenant, the Chrysler Corporation. In the 1950s Chrysler lost control of the building. Cooper Union, a private college, owns the land and leases it out. The Abu Dhabi Investment Council now controls 75 percent.

Law and Order

INTERNATIONAL EDICTS

In Hong Kong, a betrayed wife is legally allowed to kill her adulterous husband, but may only do so with her bare hands. The husband's lover may be killed in any manner desired.

In Santa Cruz, Bolivia, it is illegal for a man to have sex with a woman and her daughter at the same time.

In seventeenth-century Japan, no citizen was allowed to leave the country, on penalty of death. Anyone caught coming or going without permission was executed on the spot.

Muslims are banned from looking at the genitals of a corpse. The organs of the deceased must be covered at all times.

Caesar banned all wheeled vehicles from Rome during daylight hours.

In Scotland, all people of nobility are free from all arrests for debts, as they are the king's hereditary counselors. They cannot be outlawed in any civil action, and no attachment lies against their persons.

During the reign of Catherine I of Russia, the rules for parties stipulated that no man was to get drunk before nine o'clock, and ladies were not to get drunk at any hour.

Russia attempted to pass a law in 2008 declaring being an emo kid illegal and banning goth and emo dress styles in the hope of curbing teen depression and suicide.

It was against the law to tie a male horse next to a female horse on Main Street in Wetaskiwin, Canada, in 1917.

In France, Napoleon instituted a scale of fines for sex offenses, which included 35 francs for a man guilty of lifting a woman's skirt to the knee and 70 francs if he lifted it to the thigh.

Private cars were forbidden on the island of Bermuda until 1948, which explains why there are still so many bicycles there.

In Ireland, wearing a Halloween costume could result in up to one year in prison.

Married women were forbidden by law to watch, let alone compete, in the ancient Olympics, the penalty being death. The Greeks believed that the presence of wives in Olympia would defile Greece's oldest religious shrine there, although young girls were allowed in. Women who broke the rule were thrown from a nearby cliff.

Centuries ago, in London, someone drinking at a tavern had the legal right to demand to see the wine cellar to verify that the wine hadn't been watered down. Refusal by the tavern could result in severe penalties, including time in prison.

During the Renaissance, laws were passed that limited which fashions could be worn by the lower classes. Queen Elizabeth I of England did not allow commoners to wear the ruff; Florentine women of the lower class could not wear buttons of certain shapes and materials.

In Britain, in 1571, a man could be fined for not wearing a wool cap.

In Britain, a Witchcraft Act of the early 1700s identified black cats as dangerous animals to be shunned.

Murdering a traveling musician was not a serious crime in Britain during the Middle Ages.

In Greenwich, England, during the 1800s, it was unlawful to impersonate a retired person on a pension.

In 1547, British law was amended to end the practice of boiling people to death as punishment for criminal behavior.

In Britain, the law was changed in 1789 to make hanging the method of execution, instead of burning.

Upon entrance to the Bodleian Library, Oxford University requires all members to read aloud a pledge that includes an agreement to not "kindle therein any fire or flame."

In London, it is illegal to drive a car without sitting in the front seat.

In London, you will face a twenty-four-hour detainment if you are caught sticking gum under a seat on the upper deck of a bus.

Until about 150 years ago, churchgoing was required by law in Britain.

Men in the United Kingdom accused of murdering their current or ex-partners could until recently be acquitted by claiming "provocation," a term in British law that encompasses adultery and "nagging." In 2008 this defense was finally declared illegitimate.

In Britain, couples can't be legally married in the open air—venues need to have a permanent roof. Anyone marrying outdoors in the United Kingdom needs to have a secondary ceremony in a registry office to be legally wed.

Women are banned by royal decree from using hotel swimming pools in Jidda, Saudi Arabia.

Scandinavian law forbids television advertising of foods to children.

In Somalia, it has been decreed illegal to carry old chewing gum stuck on the tip of your nose.

Officials of ancient Greece decreed that mollusk shells be used as ballots, because once a vote was scratched on the shell, it couldn't be erased or altered.

In San Salvador, El Salvador, drunk drivers can be punished by death before a firing squad.

Under Norwegian law, a polar bear may be shot only if deemed a menace.

For hundreds of years, the Chinese zealously guarded the secret of sericulture; imperial law decreed death by torture to those who disclosed how to make silk.

The state of Vera Cruz, in Mexico, outlaws priests as citizens.

The penalty for conviction of smuggling in Bangladesh is the death penalty.

During the fourth century in Sparta, Greece, males over twenty years of age were required by law to eat two pounds of meat a day, as it was supposed to make a person brave.

The sale of chewing gum is outlawed in Singapore because it is a means of "tainting an environment free of dirt."

In Germany and Argentina, a screwing gesture at your head, meaning "You're crazy," is illegal when driving.

In ancient Cambodia, it was illegal to insult a rice plant.

The Germans considered *Casablanca* a propaganda film and made it illegal to show in German theaters during World War II. Even after the war, only a censored version was allowed to be shown in Germany, with all references to Nazis removed.

In Norway, you may not spay your female dog or cat. However, you may neuter the males of the species.

In the 1630s, Japan forbade the building of any large ocean-worthy ships, to deter defection.

In the latter part of the 1300s, dress code laws in Florence stipulated precisely the depth of a woman's décolletage.

During the fifteenth century, the handkerchief was for a time allowed only to the nobility, with special laws made to enforce this.

In Canada, if a debt is higher than 25 cents, it is illegal to pay it with pennies.

The celebration of May Day was forbidden in the time of Oliver Cromwell.

From the early 1700s to the mid 1800s, soap was considered a luxury of the British aristocracy. Those who used it were taxed.

Freelance Dutch prostitutes have to charge sales tax, but can write off items such as condoms and beds.

Around 1245, St. Albert the Great helped create a handbook for sexual penances. Punishments varied depending on the nature of the offense: anywhere from thirty days (for offenses like masturbation) to ten years (for frolicking with a cleric) of bread, water, and abstinence.

In 1999 female legislators wore jeans to Italy's parliament to protest an appeals court's dismissal of a rape conviction on the grounds it was "impossible" to rape a woman wearing jeans. The appeals court agreed with the defendant's claim that the woman had consented to sex because the jeans could not be removed without her cooperation. The ruling was finally overturned in 2008.

NATIONAL NO-NOS

Before 1933, the dime was legal as payment only in transactions of $10 or less. In that year, Congress made the dime legal tender for all transactions.

The design of a U.S. coin cannot be changed more than once in twenty-five years without special legislation by Congress.

The United States government will not allow portraits of living persons to appear on stamps.

During World War II, U.S. ice cream manufacturers were restricted by law to produce only twenty different flavors of ice cream.

Contrary to many reports, the Eisenhower Interstate System does *not* require that one mile in every five must be straight in the United States. The claim that these straight sections are usable as airstrips in times of war or other emergencies does not exist in any federal legislation. Korea and Sweden *do* use some of their roads as military airstrips.

According to U.S. law, a patent may not be granted on a useless invention or on a machine that will not operate. Even if an invention is novel or new, a patent may not be obtained if the invention would have been obvious to a person having ordinary skill in the same area at the time of the invention.

It was only after John F. Kennedy was assassinated that Congress enacted a law making it a federal crime to kill, kidnap, or assault the president, vice president, or president-elect.

In 1832, a law was passed requiring all American citizens to spend one day each year fasting and praying. People ignored the law, and no effort was made to enforce the legislation.

The Supreme Court once ruled federal income tax unconstitutional as it was not issued among the states in conformity. It was first imposed during the Civil War as a temporary revenue-raising measure.

In the United States, federal law states that children's TV shows may contain only ten minutes of advertising per hour, and on weekends the limit is ten and a half minutes.

Various states have laws prohibiting certain forms of oral sex, with penalties ranging from hefty fines to life in prison.

The states of Vermont, Alaska, Hawaii, and Maine do not allow billboards.

Connecticut and Rhode Island never ratified the Eighteenth Amendment: Prohibition.

Candy made from pieces of barrel cactus is illegal in the United States, to protect the species.

It is illegal to marry the spouse of a grandparent in Maine, Maryland, South Carolina, and Washington, DC.

IN ALABAMA . . .

Boogers may not be flicked into the wind.

It is illegal to impersonate any type of minister, of any religion.

Putting salt on a railroad track may be punishable by death.

It is illegal for a driver to be blindfolded while operating a vehicle.

It is illegal to wear a fake moustache that causes laughter in church.

Incestuous marriages are legal.

Dominoes may not be played on Sunday.

In the event of a divorce, women are entitled to keep any and all possessions that they acquired prior to the marriage, but no such allowance is made for the man.

IN ALASKA . . .

Moose may not be viewed from a plane.

It is illegal in the town of Fairbanks to feed alcoholic beverages to a moose.

IN ARIZONA . . .

It is unlawful to refuse a person a glass of water.

Donkeys cannot sleep in bathtubs.

Any misdemeanor committed while wearing a red mask is considered a felony. This goes back to the days of the Wild West.

You may not have more than two dildos in a house.

When being attacked by a criminal or burglar, you may only protect yourself with the same weapon that the other person possesses.

A hunting license is required by law to hunt rattlesnakes, but not to own them as pets.

In some smaller towns it is illegal to wear suspenders.

IN ARKANSAS . . .

Alligators may not be kept in bathtubs.

IN CALIFORNIA . . .

It was once illegal to serve alcohol to a known homosexual.

The California Board of Equalization has ruled that bartenders cannot be held responsible for misjudging the age of midgets.

In animal shelters, lizards and snakes are treated under the same guidelines as cats and dogs.

It is illegal to tether a dog for more than three hours each day.

It is a misdemeanor to shoot at any kind of game from a moving vehicle, unless the target is a whale.

LSD was legal until 1966.

On Santa Catalina, unlike the rest of Southern California, the number of cars on the island is strictly limited. The waiting time for a car permit is ten years, so most residents drive electric-powered golf carts.

In Pacific Grove, it is a misdemeanor to kill a butterfly.

In Riverside, it is illegal to kiss, unless both people wipe their lips with rose water.

IN COLORADO . . .

Car dealers may not show cars on a Sunday.

It is illegal to ride a horse while under the influence.

The letter combination JEB is banned from license plates because it's short for Jezebel. Also forbidden are 260 other three-letter combinations, including WTF, HOE, PIG, and HAG.

IN CONNECTICUT . . .

No one may use a white cane unless he or she is blind.

In order for a pickle to officially be considered a pickle, it must bounce.

You can be stopped by the police for cycling more than 65 miles per hour.

In Atwoodville, it is illegal to play Scrabble while waiting for a politician to speak.

IN FLORIDA . . .

You are not allowed to break more than three dishes per day, or chip the edges of more than four cups and/or saucers.

If an elephant is left tied to a parking meter, the parking fee has to be paid just as it would for a vehicle.

It is illegal to skateboard without a license.

It is illegal to block any traveled wagon road.

The penalty for horse theft is death by hanging.

Having sexual relations with a porcupine is illegal.

It is illegal to release more than ten lighter-than-air balloons at a time. This is to protect marine creatures that often mistake balloons for food and can suffer intestinal injuries if they eat the balloons.

It is illegal to litter intentionally with plastic fishing gear or lines.

Christmas caroling is banned at two major malls in Pensacola, as shoppers and shopkeepers complained that the carolers were too loud and took up too much space.

IN GEORGIA . . .

It is illegal to use profanity in front of a dead body lying in a funeral home or in a coroner's office.

Signs are required to be written in English as English is the state's official language.

You have the right to commit simple battery if provoked by "fighting" words.

Members of the state assembly cannot be ticketed for speeding while the state assembly is in session.

In Gwinnett County, it is illegal for residents to keep rabbits as pets, with rabbits restricted to farm areas and homes with at least three acres of land. However, the law was amended in 1993 to allow Vietnamese potbellied pigs as pets after a woman with a pet pig pleaded for the exemption.

Within the city limits of Flowery Branch, it is against the law to yell out, "Snake!"

IN HAWAII . . .

It is illegal to "annoy, molest, kill, wound, chase, shoot, or throw missiles" at a bird in any city park of Honolulu.

Coins are not allowed to be placed in a person's ears.

IN IDAHO . . .

You may not fish on a camel's back.

Riding a merry-go-round on Sundays is considered a crime.

IN ILLINOIS . . .

You may be convicted of a Class 4 felony offense, punishable by up to three years in state prison, for the crime of "eavesdropping" on a person with whom you are having a conversation.

A law prohibits barbers from using their fingers to apply shaving cream to a patron's face.

In Winnetka, while you are in a theater, it is against the law to remove your shoes if your feet smell bad.

IN INDIANA . . .

You may not back into a parking spot, because it prevents police officers from seeing your license plate.

> You are not allowed to carry a cocktail from the bar to a table. The waiter or waitress has to do it.

Baths may not be taken between the months of October and March.

> No one may catch a fish with their bare hands.

It is illegal for a liquor store to sell cold soft drinks.

> If any person has a puppet show, wire dancing, or tumbling act and receives money for it, he or she will be fined $3 under the Act to Prevent Certain Immoral Practices.

A $3 fine per pack will be imposed on anyone playing cards, under the Act for the Prevention of Gaming.

> Anyone the age of fourteen or older who profanely curses, damns, or swears by the name of God, Jesus Christ, or the Holy Ghost shall be fined between $1 and $3 for each offense, with a maximum fine of $10 per day.

Drinks on the house are illegal.

Hotel sheets must be exactly ninety-nine inches long and eighty-one inches wide.

Mustaches are illegal if the bearer has a tendency to habitually kiss other humans.

Smoking in the state legislature building is banned, except when the legislature is in session.

IN IOWA . . .

Kisses may last for no more than five minutes.

A man with a mustache may never kiss a woman in public.

One-armed piano players must perform free of charge.

It is illegal to sell or distribute drugs or narcotics without having first obtained the appropriate Iowa drug tax stamp.

In Fort Madison, the fire department is required to practice firefighting for fifteen minutes before attending a fire.

IN KANSAS . . .

Pedestrians crossing the highways at night must wear taillights.

If two trains meet on the same track, neither shall proceed until the other has passed.

In Natoma, it's illegal to throw knives at men wearing striped suits.

IN KENTUCKY . . .

All bees entering the state shall be accompanied by certificates of health, stating that the apiary from which the bees came was free from contagious or infectious disease.

It is illegal to fish with a bow and arrow.

It is illegal to fish in the Ohio River without an Indiana fishing license.

The Kentucky Supreme Court has ruled that the prosecution must throw its files wide open to the defense if the accused is suffering from amnesia.

It is against the law to throw eggs at a public speaker.

IN LOUISIANA . . .

Biting someone with your natural teeth is "simple assault," while biting someone with your false teeth is "aggravated assault."

It is illegal to gargle in public places.

It is illegal to rob a bank and then shoot at the bank teller with a water pistol.

In New Orleans, it is illegal for anyone claiming to be a palm reader, fortune-teller, or mystic healer to offer up marriage services (they are also not allowed to proclaim their ability to contact your dead or lost relatives, locate buried treasure, or predict the outcome of a lawsuit).

IN MAINE . . .

You will be charged a fine if you still have your Christmas decorations up after January 14.

Shotguns are required to be taken to church in the event of a Native American attack.

You may not step out of a plane in flight.

IN MASSACHUSETTS . . .

No gorilla is allowed in the backseat of any car.

Snoring is prohibited unless all bedroom windows are closed and securely locked.

It is illegal to go to bed without first having a full bath.

Taxi drivers are prohibited from making love in the front seat of their taxi during their shifts.

It is unlawful to injure a football goalpost. Doing so is punishable by a $200 fine.

Bullets may not be used as currency.

It is illegal to allow someone to use stilts while working on the construction of a building.

Affiliation with the Communist Party is illegal.

Tomatoes may not be used in the production of clam chowder.

Public boxing matches are outlawed.

It is illegal to drive Texan, Mexican, Cherokee, or other American Indian cattle on a public road.

Mourners may eat no more than three sandwiches during a wake.

In the seventeenth century, smoking was legal only at a distance of five miles from any town.

In 1845, Boston banned bathing unless you had a doctor's prescription. .

It is illegal to keep a mule on the second floor of a building not in a city, unless there are two exits.

IN MARYLAND . . .

It is illegal to sell condoms from vending machines, with one exception: condoms may be dispensed from a vending machine only in places where alcoholic beverages are sold for consumption on the premises.

IN MICHIGAN . . .

There is a bounty for each rat's head brought into a town office.

It is legal for a robber to file a lawsuit if he or she got hurt in your house.

Any person over the age of twelve may have a license for a handgun, as long as he or she has not been convicted of a felony.

A woman isn't allowed to cut her own hair without her husband's permission.

IN MINNESOTA . . .

Citizens may not enter Wisconsin with a chicken on their head.

All men driving motorcycles must wear shirts.

All bathtubs must have feet.

IN MISSISSIPPI . . .

Horses are not to be housed within fifty feet of any road.

IN MISSOURI . . .

In St. Louis, it is illegal to drink beer out of a bucket while you're sitting on a curb.

IN MONTANA . . .

It is illegal for married women to go fishing alone on Sundays, and illegal for unmarried women to fish alone at all.

It is a misdemeanor to show movies that depict acts of felonious crime.

It is illegal to have a sheep in the cab of your truck without a chaperone.

It is a felony for a wife to open her husband's mail.

Seven or more American Indians are considered a raiding or war party, and it is legal to shoot them.

A couple can get married even if neither of them is present for the ceremony, if two proxies will show up and recite the vows in their place.

IN NEBRASKA . . .

It is illegal for a mother to give her daughter a perm without a state license.

It is illegal to go whale fishing.

IN NEVADA . . .

The removal and possession of cacti and Christmas trees are regulated.

It is still "legal" to hang someone for shooting your dog on your property.

It is illegal to drive a camel on the highway.

In December 1997, the first legislation was passed categorizing Y2K data disasters as "acts of God"— protecting the state from lawsuits that might potentially have been brought against it by residents in the year 2000.

In Las Vegas, it is against the law to pawn your dentures.

IN NEW HAMPSHIRE . . .

You cannot sell the clothes you are wearing to pay off a gambling debt.

It is illegal to pick up seaweed off the beach.

On Sundays, citizens may not relieve themselves while looking up.

IN NEW JERSEY . . .

You cannot pump your own gas. All gas stations are full service only.

All motorists must honk, or give "audible warning," before passing another vehicle.

It is illegal to wear a bulletproof vest while committing a murder.

It is against the law to frown at a police officer.

You may not slurp your soup.

Spray paint may not be sold without a posted sign warning juveniles of the penalty for creating graffiti.

IN NEW MEXICO . . .

State officials once demanded four hundred words of "sexually explicit material" be cut from *Romeo and Juliet*.

It is against the law to ship horned toads out of the state.

IN NEW YORK . . .

It is against the law to throw a ball at someone's head for fun.

A license must be purchased before hanging clothes on a clothesline.

It is illegal to shoot a rabbit from a moving trolley car.

In New York City, in 1908 a law was passed making it illegal for women to smoke in public.

In New York City, it is illegal to make your living through the skinning of horses or cows, the growing of ragweed, or the burning of bones.

IN NORTH CAROLINA . . .

It became illegal to plow a field with an elephant after circus showman P. T. Barnum created a spectacle when he hitched an elephant to a plow beside the train tracks to announce that his circus had come to town.

It's against the law to "pretend" to be married when registering for a hotel room. On the other hand, if the couple checking into the honeymoon suite is legitimately hitched but can't "close the deal" due to one or both parties being sexually impotent, the marriage can be declared null and void.

IN NORTH DAKOTA . . .

It is legal to shoot an American Indian on horseback, provided you are in a covered wagon.

IN OHIO . . .

In Sandusky, anyone older than age fourteen looking for goodies on Halloween is breaking the law.

IN PENNSYLVANIA . . .

The law mandates that each year all counties provide veterans' graves with flags, most of which are distributed before Memorial Day.

In Hazelton, it is illegal to sip a carbonated drink while lecturing students in a school auditorium.

IN RHODE ISLAND . . .

In Providence, no store is allowed to sell a toothbrush on the Sabbath. Yet these same stores are allowed to sell toothpaste and mouthwash on Sundays.

IN SOUTH CAROLINA . . .

Merchandise may not be sold within a half mile of a church, unless it is fruit being sold.

> If a man over sixteen proposes marriage to an unwed woman without actually intending to marry her, he's guilty of a misdemeanor. However, he's off the hook if he can demonstrate that at the time of the alleged seduction the woman was behaving "lewd and un-chaste."

IN SOUTH DAKOTA . . .

In the town of Spearfish, if three or more American Indians are walking down the street together, they can be considered a war party and fired upon.

IN TENNESSEE . . .

It was only in 1968 that the state abolished its anti-evolution law and accepted the doctrine of evolution.

In South Pittsburg, also known as the "Cornbread

Capital of the World," a law concerning the cooking of this Southern staple declares: "Cornbread isn't cornbread unless it be made correctly. Therefore, all cornbread must be hereby made in nothing other then a cast-iron skillet. Those found in violation of this ordinance are to be fined one dollar."

IN TEXAS . . .

A bill was passed in 1997 to allow absentee ballots to be cast from space. The first to exercise this right to vote while in orbit was astronaut David Wolf, who cast his vote for Houston mayor via e-mail from the Russian space station *Mir* in November 1997.

A man can beat his wife as long as he doesn't use an object larger than his thumb.